Notes on Meditation

Notes on MEDITATION

by

Allan Armstrong ODP

Foreword

Andrew Francis

IMAGIER PUBLISHING
BRISTOL 2011

First published in 2011 by
Imagier Publishing
Rookery Farm
Bristol BS35 3SY
United Kingdom
Email: ip@imagier.com
www.imagier.com

ISBN 13: 978-0-9558415-7-6

Cover and text design by Allan Armstrong
The paper used in this publication is from a sustainable source and is elemental chlorine free.

Printed and bound by CPI Group (UK) Ltd, Croydon, CR0 4YY

Contents

Illustrations vi

Preface vii

Foreword 9

Introductory Notes 15

Module 1 – The Chemistry of Stress 26

Module 2 – The Mechanics of Meditation 44

Module 3 – Concentrating the Mind 56

Module 4 – Controlled Imagining 69

Module 5 – The Art of Meditation 94

Module 6 – Therapeutic Meditation 115

Conclusion 123

Illustrations

Frontis, *A Solitary in Lectio*

Flowchart 14

Fig. 1 Hypothalamus 28

Fig. 2 Endocrinal & Autonomic Nervous System 29

Fig. 3 Endocrinal Glands 33

Fig. 4 Brainwaves 42

Fig. 5 Normal Beta State 42

Fig. 6 Heightened Beta state 42

Fig. 7 Left & Right Brain Modes 63

Fig. 8 Force-field Analysis 64

Fig. 9 Priority Management Matrix 64

Fig. 10 ODP Curriculum Mindmap 67

Fig. 11 Exercise 1 83

Fig. 12 Exercise 2 84

Fig. 13 Exercise 3 85

Fig. 14 Exercise 4 86

Fig. 15 Exercise 5 87

Fig. 16 Transient Self I 90

Fig. 17 Transient Self II 93

Preface

Notes on Meditation is one of a series of books describing the life and work of the Order of Dionysis and Paul, a religious order of men and women committed to following the contemplative life whilst living in the secular world. The mission of the Order of Dionysis and Paul is to assist those who seek to enter the 'Presence of God' by instructing them in the spiritual disciplines of Prayer and Meditation.

The bulk of the material contained within this small volume is concerned with important biological and psycho-dynamic factors that stand as obstacles in the way of being effective in meditation, and provides simple methods and techniques that enable the student to recognise, understand and overcome such obstacles and harness the extraordinary powers of the mind and soul.

This book is designed and set out as a series of modules that may be undertaken either by an individual, or used in a group setting, and requires no further knowledge than is contained within each module. The work is self-explanatory and easy to engage with, however, it should be recognised that the information given herein consists of notes only and does not pretend in any way to be definitive. Within the Order of Dionysis and Paul members are encouraged to study in greater depth the subject-matter addressed in the modules. Furthermore, withinin the Order this work is generally undertaken with the assistance of a spiritual director – that is, with the assistance of one who is both proficient and knowledgeable in this work, thereby providing students with an experienced guide and a focal point for advice concerning issues arising in meditation.

The exercises contained herein are not in themselves objectives but the means by which effective meditation may be achieved. They are essentially a beginning, a beginning of a journey of self-knowledge and should be approached as such; simply reading the text will not give the ability to meditate effectively. Within the Order of Dionysis and Paul it is accepted that meditation is more than a rational comprehension of something, such as in grasping the meaning of a sentence; it is an act of will, of committing oneself to fully engaging with the interior life of the soul and the chemistry of consciousness taking place therein, and the modules contained in this book are designed to enable the student to control and transcend that chemistry rather than being controlled by it. For it is what takes place when that chemistry is recognised, understood and sublimated in the fires of the spiritual life that makes meditation such a powerful and amazing tool.

Those committed enough to work their way through these modules, who are sufficiently motivated to return again and again to the exercises set out therein, to engage with them and to study them in depth, will achieve great things in the field of the inner life.

Allan Armstrong ODP
Bristol 2011

Foreword

In a world of economic turbulence, ecological fragility, shifting moral values and rampant secularism, to be able to focus upon that which is truly important, to centre and harmonise one's own being, is vital, life-giving and necessary. Therefore, to receive the means to achieve this is a valuable gift. Meditation is one such gift which enables the individual to focus upon the truly important, to focus upon centring one's own being. This consists of an inward journey – a journey that is spoken of by all spiritual masters – a journey, moreover, that always involves meditation. Many will claim to offer such a gift but few can impart it with care and certainty.

Yet the word 'meditation' carries many connotations. These come from both popular culture and the richest faith traditions. Thus, the Beatles went to India for a few weeks to learn from the Guru Mahesh Yogi, while Tibetan Buddhists encourage people to spend years learning to meditate. New Age centres from Scotland to the Greek islands enjoin participants to share in daily times of meditation and Sufi mystics commit themselves to the lifelong development of the practices of *dhikr* (repeating the names of God to focus upon him) and *muraqaba* or meditation. Whether at melas or rock festivals, the yurts and tipis appear as meditation centres, with floor cushions, ambient music and incense –

but with little guidance. Christian contemplatives, from the second-century Desert Fathers and Celtic saints to the present day, show that it is a disciplined approach to the spiritual life which will bring both the greatest peace and deepest discernment. Despite the evident search for meaning there is in this country a growing suspicion of institutional religion – a suspicion reflected tellingly in the growth of weekly 'meditation' classes in local community centres. The counterpoint between populist froth and those richest faith traditions indicates that a new approach to meditation is needed – as the contrasting examples above clearly demonstrate.

Too often the word, and more importantly the practice of 'meditation' is devalued by insufficient teaching about the nature of its very practice. To take but one example amongst many, there is within contemporary evangelical Christianity far too much exhortation for a daily 'waiting upon the Word', with little instruction about how one should approach that time of quiet in God's acknowledged presence. This and other examples must not devalue or expunge the practice of meditation, as previous centuries' critics of the Quietist tradition often sought to do. However, for many from the Christian tradition it is historically within monasticism, or in more recent times within the Quaker movement, that silence and meditation has been utilised as part of a life-long involvement with the spiritual life.

So this book is an encouragement as it clearly shows how the practice of true meditation can be nurtured, to enrich the everyday. Nor should it be dismissed as simply a manual merely because each of its chapters acts as a module for personal growth in one's own meditation. These chapters or modules reveal how both physiology and posture affect our ability to focus, and offer both practical guidance and patterns to aid our spiritual and meditative growth. On the way, we can learn of the strength gained in deepening our inward journey. What becomes obvious is that true meditation has a qualitative nature rather than the quantitative approach which initially and vacuously catapults seekers into hours of meditation, thereby diminishing the joy and gift which true meditation brings.

It is important to learn how to meditate. It is also important to learn how to meditate well, and it is especially important to learn from those who have the experience of many years and who teach with a spiritual maturity. Allan Armstrong is one such person. As the writer of this short book, Allan's wisdom appears through its very simplicity.

I come from the Anabaptist-Christian tradition, often described 'as neither Protestant nor Catholic'. Our spirituality seeks to draw on both those Christian streams, valuing the Protestant focus upon the Gospels to reveal the Lord's teaching and equally valuing Catholic foci upon the practices of prayer and community to unite God's people. My own spiritual quest has taken me across the world, encountering many, accepting all, learning from some as quiet contemplation and silence gradually form the heart of my own daily prayer. It was from the monks at Taizé in France that I first realised how much I needed to learn properly to meditate in order to appreciate Scripture and silence more fully. If only I had known Allan Armstrong then!

Allan Armstrong is the Prior of a small religious order, the Order of Dionysis and Paul, which has much in common with similar groups within the Orthodox tradition. The ODP's practice of Compline – night prayer – is built around meditation. A portion of scripture is read repeatedly at a slow pace, enhancing its meaning whilst allowing its absorption. Rarely does any member of the Order or visitor to Compline reflect upon the whole passage. Often it may just be a single verse or one of Jesus' injunctions to his followers. Sometimes, like the Sufi mystic's *dhikr*, the names of God are gently and repeatedly invoked or the Jesus Prayer is inhaled and exhaled rhythmically.

It must be emphasised that the ODP is not an enclosed Order, with its members locked away in some monastic enclave. They all live 'in the world', earning their own living and they are committed to the exercise of discipleship in their own homes and neighbourhoods. Their prayer and meditation must thus enable them to live in the pressures of today's world. And it is for this reason that this book has great value beyond the circle of ODP members. It explains how meditation can develop both personal and shared spirituality. Their generosity to visitors at Compline or Sunday Prayer is reflected in their hospitality afterwards, sharing whatever food is brought whilst listening carefully together to whoever is speaking. Their community's meditation greatly enriches their welcome to others.

As the Prior, Allan lives as other members do. He is an unpaid leader, drawing no expenses from his work in teaching seekers – a mark of his personal integrity. He is a well-read man of great spiritual depth, who rises early to pray in the quiet of his extended family's home. Together, almost weekly, we discuss many things as we share the insights from each of our respective communities. I continue to learn from Allan about meditation as 'a way of holiness' and am privileged to know him as good friend.

This book has a place in the world, and it will flow from that place if you would but let it. It may be that in the midst of life's pressures, you know that the balance of your life is not quite right even if there is not an obvious emptiness. Simply ask how you centre your own being. Do you have an answer? Whether your answer is ambiguous or certain, meditation will enrich you. Each page of this book will make that apparent – as you share the silence and grow in the practice of meditation. So this book is worth reading, using well and then commending onward to friends.

Andrew Francis
The London Mennonite Centre
September 2011

Flowchart

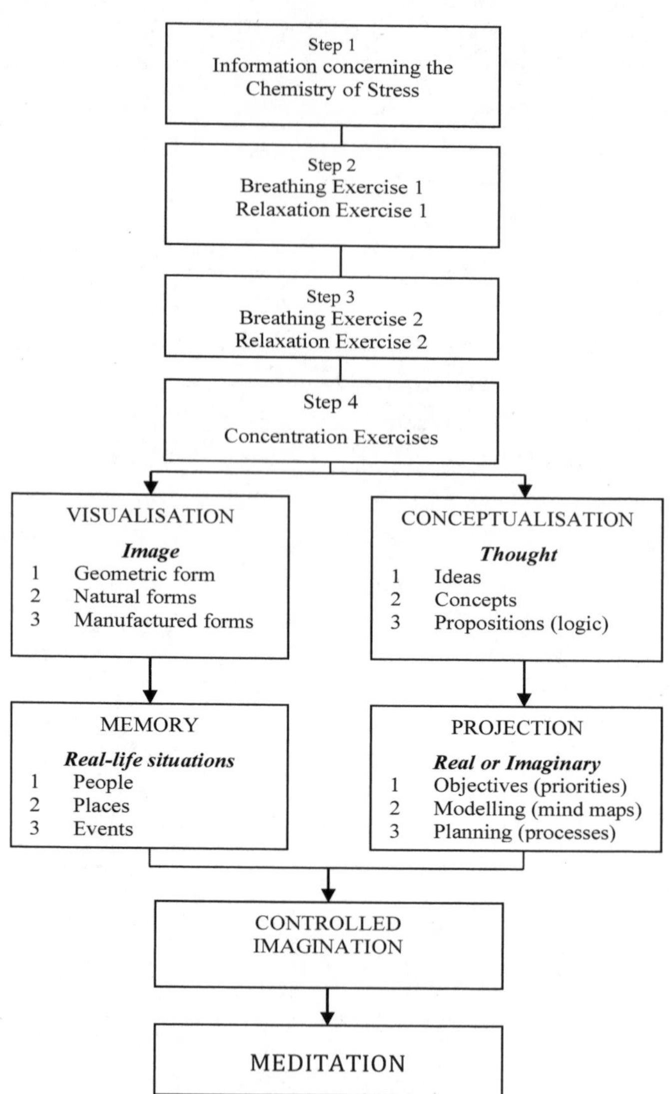

Step 1
Information concerning the Chemistry of Stress
Step 2
Breathing Exercise 1
Relaxation Exercise 1
Step 3
Breathing Exercise 2
Relaxation Exercise 2
Step 4
Concentration Exercises
VISUALISATION
Image
1 Geometric form
2 Natural forms
3 Manufactured forms
CONCEPTUALISATION
Thought
1 Ideas
2 Concepts
3 Propositions (logic)
MEMORY
Real-life situations
1 People
2 Places
3 Events
PROJECTION
Real or Imaginary
1 Objectives (priorities)
2 Modelling (mind maps)
3 Planning (processes)
CONTROLLED IMAGINATION
MEDITATION

Introductory Notes

1. The word 'Meditation' has been in circulation for ever, so it would seem, but the question remains, what is meditation? Not so difficult a question to answer one might think, but popular opinion has become confused if not divided over this question. It clearly means different things to different people, although this has not always been the case.

2. Over the course of the last forty years or so the term 'meditation' has come to mean two distinct things. On the one hand there is the traditional concept of meditation being an exercise in mind control directed towards self-knowledge and spiritual evolution, and on the other hand there is the modern concept of meditation being a therapeutic exercise in deep relaxation and active imagination directed towards inducing a sense of well-being, employed more often than not as an antidote to the stresses of modern living.

3. One side associates meditation with oriental religions and philosophies, where the archetypal image that presents itself to the imagination is of a Buddhist monk or Indian sadhu sitting cross-legged on a cushion or low wooden stool, eyes closed and breathing slowly; possibly chanting or repeating a mantra. The other side associates meditation with relaxation and creative visualisation, where a typical image that presents itself is of a person relaxing in a comfortable

reclining chair, listening to ambient music and or a gentle voice describing an 'ideal' environment wherein the student allows the mind to wander

4. In recent times the most popular methods of meditation that have taken root in the modern world are themselves products of the imagination of that world. They are essentially guided imaginings deriving more from a syncretic blend of Spiritualism, Yoga, Buddhism and Shamanism, to name but a few, than from any school of traditional meditation, oriental or otherwise.

5. Most of the methods used are not derived from the ancient world, or from the Far East, but emerged in Europe and its colonies, originating in the ideas and practices employed by nineteenth and early twentieth-century esoteric schools such as the Hermetic Order of the Golden Dawn. This particular order is significant in that it became the archetypal model for the formation of a host of esoteric orders and movements, most of which were deeply involved with the magical aspects of Western esotericism – especially with astral projection and all that such implies: and it implies a great deal where modern ideas about meditation are concerned.

6. Looking back a little further, it is possible to see how in the nineteenth century the emergence of these schools was an inevitable and natural expression of the interest in Hermetic and Rosicrucian thought and philosophy that emerged in seventeenth and eighteenth-century Europe. These schools

were not only a focus for the theoretical, but also for the practical workings of Western esotericism.

7. The first half of the nineteenth century witnessed the resurgence of a form of ancestor worship in the form of Spiritualism, and the latter half of that century saw the emergence of the Theosophical Society, a movement that sought to create a universal religion based upon oriental religious ideas such as those fostered in Buddhism. This point is particularly significant because it was through the activities of this society that Hinduism and Buddhism, particularly Tibetan Buddhism, became so accessible to popular culture in the West.

8. The high point of the Theosophical Society was during the 1920's and 1930's. However, as was the case for many social movements of that time, the society's growth and development was impeded by the drama of the Second World War. Curiously, as the world began its slow recovery from the effects of that dreadful war public interest in the Theosophical Society began to fade. A paradoxical if not ironic turn of events because it was at this time that popular interest in Hindu systems of yoga and meditation, nurtured by the Theosophical Society, began to grow in popularity.

9. Shamanism, on the other hand, did not emerge in popular Western culture until the late twentieth century, and then only in a romanticised form: its popularity, perhaps, being due to its association with chemically induced states of mind conducive to 'astral projection' and 'channelling'; subjects that

have either fascinated or horrified humanity from the earliest times. Exploring significant or interesting environments or worlds through the realm of the imagination is not a new thing; it has been around a long time but the emphasis on it is certainly a modern phenomenon.

10. Another significant contribution to the guided imagination approach has come from the various psychodynamic processes that surfaced, particularly in America, from the mid-twentieth century onward. Although deeply influenced by the materialism of analytical psychology and behaviourism, and invariably defined in the psychological language of Freud, Jung and their successors, they are often to be found at the heart of many modern systems of spirituality and self-development.

11. Another dimension in modern thinking about meditation is the concept of 'endorphins'. These are small, protein molecules produced by cells in the body that work to relieve pain with sedative receptors found in the brain, spinal cord and nerve endings. They come in several forms and are many times more powerful than any pharmaceutical analgesic. Endorphins are understood to relieve pain, to enhance the immune system and to reduce stress but, more significantly, especially from the point of view of this discussion, they induce an enhanced feeling of well-being.

12. There are several methods known to stimulate the body's production of endorphins including acupuncture,

shiatsu, massage, creative visualisation and a variety of relaxation techniques. Many of these methods are now promoted under the banner of meditation. Consequently, in the popular culture of the Western world, meditation has become synonymous with the practice of guided imagining directed towards evoking an experience of bliss and well-being. Nevertheless, as valuable as such tools may be, especially in a therapeutic sense, they have little in common with the objectives and disciplines of traditional meditation. The natural 'high' that may occur in traditional meditation, however welcome, is not in itself the main objective but a by-product of the main endeavour, which is invariably self-knowledge and or union with God.

13. To understand what traditional meditation actually is one must be prepared to peel away the many layers of preconceptions surrounding it in the modern world. A common theme in the secular world is that like all things in our civilisation the art of meditation has evolved in line with our growing understanding of the world – that we have outgrown the traditional approach with all of its outmoded religious connotations – and that the old must give way to the new.

14. Alternatively, we may recognise that traditional meditation is an ancient method of self-enquiry conceived and designed to engage with the underlying reality of existence, a reality that is eternal and changeless and thus beyond biological need or the ambitions of society.

15. This traditional perspective may be a radical point of view in modern terms, however, it should be noted that from a traditional and classical point of view meditation has long been understood to be a private and introspective discipline of applied thought whereby, in a chemical free state of deep relaxation, the faculties of the mind are concentrated upon a given theme or subject. In short, traditional meditation is mind control through thinking about a given subject.

16. In the precincts of the sanctuary, wherein traditional meditation evolved, the subject matter to be meditated upon was usually, although not always, derived from sacred texts. Thus in Buddhism the theme was generally taken from the various writings that constitute the Dharma and the life of the Buddha. In Vedanta the theme would be drawn from the Vedas or the Upanishads, and in the Christian world the theme would usually be drawn from the Scriptures and the life of Christ.

17. The simple act of thinking deeply about a given subject constitutes the core discipline of traditional meditation. The mind does not necessarily have to be focussed upon religious or spiritual themes but it should be noted that the discipline of traditional meditation did evolve within the precincts of the sanctuary and has been nurtured therein for as long any one can tell. In those environs meditating, or thinking deeply about spiritual themes, establishes the context for the student to engage with the fundamental questions of existence, such as, 'Who am I?' and 'What is the purpose of life?' It begins as an exercise in reasoning, but gradually becomes an inward

journey of self-knowledge where reason, being inadequate for the task, is displaced by intuition. It is a discipline that is initially difficult to learn, but once learnt has surprising and often sublime results.

18. An interesting feature of the sacred texts of the world is that they have many levels of meaning embedded within them. From the earliest times symbols, metaphors and allegories were widely employed by those who created these texts. Such devices may not serve those who choose to look at them as literal or mythical accounts of the distant past but, for those who approach them with an open mind, symbols, metaphors and allegories often serve as keys to the spiritual wisdom and understanding contained therein. Spiritual teachings are often presented in the form of stories or myths; indeed, the Bible may be seen as a collection of such stories, stories that many accept as true historical accounts.

19. Whether historically true or not the sacred texts do conceal great spiritual truths that were clearly thought too profound for the spiritually naïve and many subtleties were employed in maintaining and safeguarding them; their composition being designed in such a way that they could be discussed and interpreted on different levels, depending on the level of understanding of the student, each giving a different or deeper insight to the story.

20. Philo Judaeus, who lived in the Egyptian city of Alexandria during the first century AD, wrote extensively about the allegorical interpretation of the Scriptures. Much

later, Moses de Leon, who lived during the late thirteenth century, likened the Scriptures to a nut with a shell of literal meaning on the outside and an essential or mystical meaning within. He summed up his understanding of this in the word 'PARDeS', which means Garden or Paradise – alluding to an illumined mind. The word is a cipher concealing an esoteric understanding of existence. Each consonant of this word refers to a method of extrapolating meaning; thus P represents the literal meaning; R represents the allegorical meaning, particularly in the moral sense; D represents the metaphorical meaning, particularly in the symbolic sense, and S stands for the mystical meaning. Arthur Edward Waite, a celebrated English mystic of the late nineteenth and early twentieth centuries, describing the same thing, said that P equals the literal, R the symbolic, D the allegorical, and finally S equals the mystical sense.

21. Over the centuries many different systems of traditional meditation have emerged, many of which are based on the premise that the discursive activities of the mind may be brought to a standstill by focussing the attention on one subject to the exclusion of all others, thereby revealing the true and permanent reality underpinning all things.

22. Although this premise is essentially true, a common mistake is made by some of those engaging in traditional meditation in assuming that one should avoid trying to think when meditating, but trying not to think is like trying not to breathe, almost impossible. The truth is, and it is a truth that

has long been understood in the precincts of the sanctuary, that there is a point in the cycle of meditation when the discursive activities of the mind pause or cease, an event that may be facilitated by focussing the attention on one subject; but it is a place one arrives at, not a place one starts from.

23. To focus on the breath is a means of stilling the biochemistry of the body, thereby slowing down the mental and emotional activity of the mind. It is the first stage of meditation and has been universally employed in this manner for as long as any can tell. To concentrate the mind on a significant concept or idea is the second stage, although both may be initiated simultaneously.

24. In the schools wherein spiritual development is the primary objective the focal point of concentration is usually the Scriptures, to which the wandering attention is always returned. However, this activity, no matter how rewarding it may be in terms of inspiration, is not the ultimate objective; meditation is not an endless path of cerebral activity, nor is it an endless state of emptiness.

25. Like all things in the natural world there is a cycle of activity which the traditional schools have come to understand and to which they adhere. That natural cycle, most obvious in the rotation of the seasons, consists of directing the mind towards a single activity that results, eventually, in a form of realisation culminating in a period of profound stillness.

26. Meditation is not in itself the objective but a means of achieving the objective. For those who persevere on this path the discipline of meditation leads the student into the exalted and sublime state of Contemplation, wherein the mysteries of existence are slowly revealed to the maturing student. This is the main objective of traditional meditation.

27. The term 'meditation' has then, in recent times, come to signify two different undertakings. The first is traditional meditation, which is a method of mind control that from the earliest times has been directed towards self-knowledge and spiritual insight.

28. The second is a modern concept of meditation, which is a therapeutic method with many variations that is directed towards inducing a sense of well-being as an antidote to the stresses of modern living, focussing upon the use of the imagination as a means of inducing the desired effect.

29. The modern concept of meditation is also applied in certain schools in the development of psychic abilities and skills, such as astral projection and clairvoyance. As such it no longer falls under the heading of meditation and arguably should go by a different name as it has little in common with meditation in general.

30. This is not to criticise such undertakings. I cannot speak for such schools as I am not privy to their councils, and by the same token I cannot speak against them. Nevertheless I do

think it important to make a distinction between them and their very different objectives from traditional and modern therapeutic methods.

31. Traditional meditation, with its focus on mind control and self-knowledge, is fundamentally different from the majority of modern meditational systems which are therapeutic in nature and focussed upon creative imagination, and both of these differ from the psychically dynamic processes presented in certain schools as meditation.

32. If there is any confusion in making a distinction between them it must inevitably rest in the fact that although they all share certain ideas and processes in common, the objectives and the application of such processes vary greatly.

33. Consequently, the student who seeks union with the Divine will be better served following the path of traditional meditation in whatever school they are led to. Alternatively, the student who is looking for respite from the stresses and strains of the world will be better served undertaking a modern method involving creative imagination etc. Those who are called to the magical arts will inevitably gravitate to the school most suitable to their temperament.

It remains for me to say that the following pages contain information and exercises that may be useful to students interested in all of the aforementioned types of meditation.

Module 1 – The Chemistry of Stress

Anyone seeking to become proficient in the art of meditation must initially acquire two basic skills, first in relaxation, because effective meditation requires a stable biological platform, and second in concentration, because it is through concentration that we overcome the transient activities of our mind. Not an easy task, but not unachievable; indeed for most of us, achieving a state of relaxation stable enough for the practice of meditation would be greatly improved if we were to understand the impact that everyday tension and stress has upon the chemistry of the body and how we think. The following notes are included to hopefully assist in this objective.

Tension & Stress

At a molecular level matter exists in a natural and fluid state of tension that is established upon electromagnetic forces of attraction and repulsion. When the tension changes the effect can be intensely powerful, that is to say, stressful. In terms of human experience stress is usually associated with an increase rather than a decrease in tension, and certain situations are commonly understood to increase tension and produce stress, for example:

- The death of someone close
- Divorce or separation
- Moving home
- Work insecurity
- Financial insecurity
- Health problems
- Increase in responsibilities
- Domestic strife
- Poor performance at work
- Child care issues

The Fight/Flight Mechanism

Our ability to survive is based upon our ability to respond to real or imagined threats. Our response to threatening situations is usually either to fight or run away, to deal with them or run away, and is consequently known as the fight/flight mechanism; it is our instinctive response to danger. This mechanism is governed by the hypothalamus, which is a controlling gland in the centre of our brain. It is the primary link between the endocrinal glandular system and the autonomic nervous system. It directs the 'fight or flight' response to danger via the autonomic nervous system.

The Autonomic Nervous System

The autonomic nervous system consists of the sympathetic and parasympathetic nervous systems. The sympathetic nervous system serves the fight/flight mechanism. It is the physiological base of our ability to respond and adapt to stimulation – either pain or pleasure. It controls the upper limits of physiological activity, generating a state of arousal and activity that initiates movement concerned with survival. Some of its functions include stopping digestion, opening the airways of the lungs and increasing heart rate and blood pressure.

The parasympathetic nervous system is the counterbalance to the sympathetic nervous system. It controls the lower limits of physiological activity and is responsible for maintaining and conserving the body's resources. It regulates physiological maintenance, including processes such as cell growth, digestion, relaxation and sleep. Some of the functions of this system include the storage of vital resources, promoting digestion, the distribution of nutrients, the constriction of bronchi and the slowing of respiration and the decrease of heart rate and blood pressure.

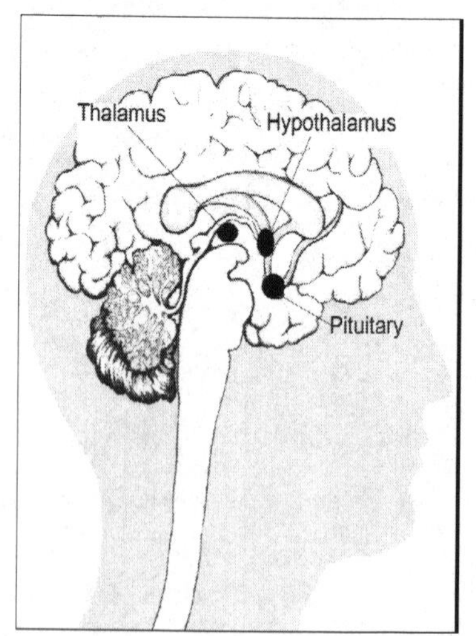

Fig. 1 Hypothalamus

Recognising how this subtle mechanism works is fundamental to our understanding of stress because it is a mechanism that is involved with every part of our life. The trigger for this mechanism is the presence of certain hormones in our system, some of which stimulate the sympathetic

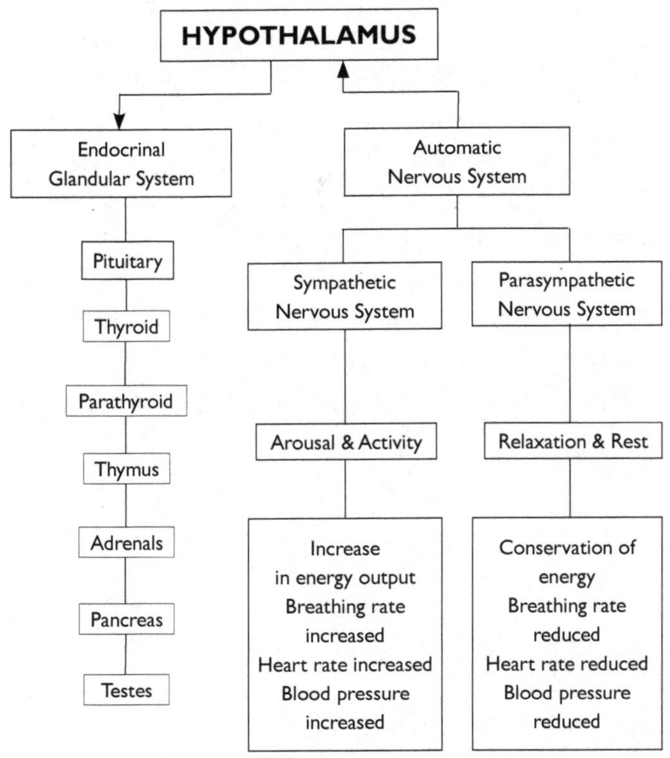

Fig. 2 Endocrinal & Autonomic Nervous Systems

nervous system to arouse the body, and others, which stimulate the parasympathetic nervous system to relax the body. Hormones are chemicals that transfer information and instructions between cells, controlling the function of various organs, and regulating metabolism, which is the process of converting food into energy. Unlike information sent via the nervous system, which is transmitted very quickly and has an immediate and short-term effect, hormones generally act more slowly and their affects are felt over a longer period of time. It is the endocrinal glandular system that produces most of these hormones, and it is the hypothalamus that controls the endocrines by emitting chemicals that either stimulate or suppress hormone secretions from the pituitary gland.

Endocrine Glands

The pineal, pituitary, thyroid, parathyroid, thymus, adrenals, pancreas and Testes (ovaries or gonads) comprise the endocrine system. The hypothalamus is a gland in the brain that functions as the command centre that controls the endocrine system through the pituitary, which directs the other endocrinal glands. The pineal produces both serotonin, which plays a fundamental role in stabilising mood, and melatonin, which is central to the sleep/wake cycle (circadian cycle). The thymus is the central control organ for the immune system; the thyroid, regulates the body's metabolism and the parathyroid controls the amount of calcium and phosphate in the bloodstream. The pancreas secretes insulin, which regulates the level of sugar in the bloodstream, and the gonads regulate sexual development, ovulation, and growth of sex organs. All play an essential role in maintaining good health, and are the subject of a great deal of very interesting scientific enquiry; however, it is one particular function of the adrenal glands that concerns us. The adrenal glands produce adrenaline and cortisol; these are hormones which arouses the body to respond to unexpected events and emergencies; speeding up our heart rate, breathing rate, blood pressure and metabolism. Blood vessels open wider to let more blood flow to the muscles. Pupils dilate to improve vision, and the liver releases stored glucose to increase the body's energy. These physical changes prepare us to handle not only the occasional dangers we may encounter, but also many of the pressures we may meet in our daily life.

Notes on Hormones

Hormones are made by specialized glands or tissues, the majority of which are produced by the glands of the endocrine system. These glands produce and secrete hormones directly into the bloodstream. Not all hormones are produced by endocrine glands. Some are produced by the mucous membranes of the small intestine, stimulating the secretion of digestive juices. Hormones are also produced in the placenta, an organ formed during pregnancy, to regulate aspects of foetal development.

Most hormones are released directly into the bloodstream, where they circulate throughout the body in very low concentrations. Hormones significantly affect the activity of every cell in the body. They influence mental acuity, physical agility, body build and stature. For example, growth hormone is a hormone produced by the pituitary gland. It regulates growth by stimulating the formation of bone and the uptake of amino acids, molecules vital to building muscle and other tissue. Sex hormones regulate the development of sexual organs, sexual behaviour, reproduction, and pregnancy. Hormones also regulate blood pressure and other involuntary body functions.

Hormones are important in regulating metabolism. For example thyroxin, a hormone secreted by the thyroid gland, regulates body metabolism. Glucagon and insulin, secreted in the pancreas, control the levels of glucose in the blood and the availability of energy for the muscles. A number of hormones, including insulin, glucagon, cortisol, growth hormone, adrenaline (epinephrine) and noradrenaline

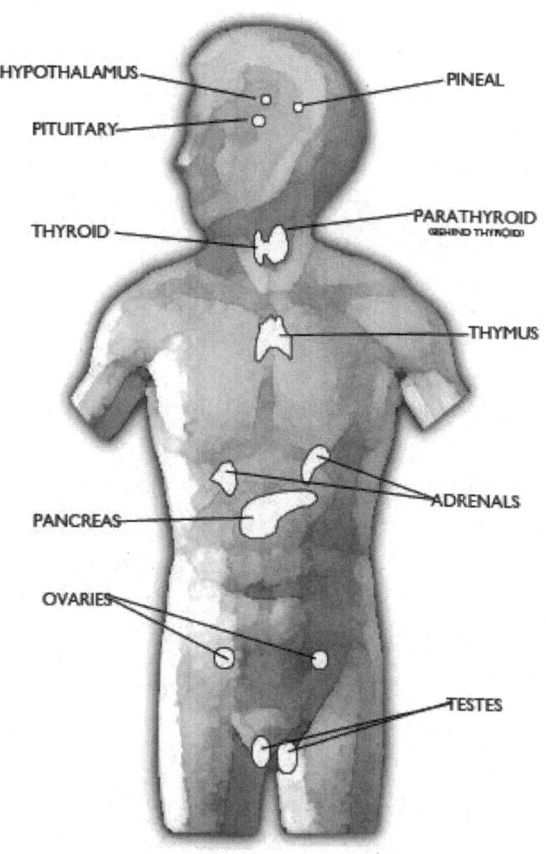

Fig. 3 Endocrinal Glands

(norepinephrine) maintain glucose levels in the blood. Insulin lowers the blood glucose whilst all the other hormones raise it. A protein called somatostatin blocks the release of insulin, glucagon and growth hormone, while another hormone, gastric inhibitory polypeptide, enhances insulin release in response to glucose absorption. This complex system permits blood glucose concentration to remain within a very narrow range, despite external conditions that may vary to extremes.

Noradrenaline and adrenaline, secreted by the adrenal medulla, affect the peripheral sympathetic nervous system: heart, blood vessels, gut, lungs, bladder and genitalia. Along with cortisol they are central to the activity of the sympathetic nervous system and the fight/flight mechanism. Noradrenaline is understood to affect mood, promoting alertness and producing changes associated with aggression and hostile behaviour. Adrenaline is associated with anxiety.

Serotonin is involved in the transmission of nerve impulses, which increases mood. It is naturally produced in the pineal gland, which produces higher levels during the summer months than in the winter months. It is involved in the control of appetite, sleep, memory and learning, temperature regulation, cardiovascular function, muscle contraction, endocrine regulation and depression. Low levels of serotonin make us vulnerable to depression, anxiety, apathy, fear, low self-esteem, insomnia and fatigue. Levels are effectively increased by antidepressants such as fluoxitine (Prozac, for example).

Endorphins are morphine like hormones synthesised by the hypothalamus and secreted into the bloodstream by the pituitary gland. Four different types of endorphin are produced in the body: Alpha, Beta, Gamma and Sigma. They behave similarly to opiates, and are strongly analgesic, stimulating an overall sense of well-being. Besides functioning as pain regulators, endorphins are also involved with physiological processes including euphoric feelings, appetite modulation and the release of sex hormones. The release of endorphins also lowers blood pressure a major indicator in heart disease.

Melatonin is a hormone produced by the pineal gland from the amino acid tryptophan. The release of melatonin is increased by darkness and reduced by light. Levels of melatonin in the blood are highest prior to bedtime. Melatonin possesses antioxidant properties. Although the most important role of melatonin is probably the circulation of sleep–wake cycle, it also has an important role in the management of metabolism, reproduction, appetite, muscular coordination and balance, and of the immune system in fighting off diseases triggered by bacteria, viruses, chemical pollutants and excessive free radical activity

Thyroxine (T4) and triiodthyronine (T3) are hormones produced by the thyroid gland, which is situated just below the larynx. The thyroid gland produces the hormones T3 and T4 by combining iodine and an amino acid called tyrosine. Both T3 and T4 are essential to the control of metabolism (the conversion of oxygen and calories to energy). Every cell in the body depends upon these hormones for the regulation of their metabolism. Problems with the thyroid occur when the gland doesn't supply the proper amount of hormones needed by the body. If the thyroid is overactive, it releases too much thyroid hormone into the bloodstream, resulting in hyperthyroidism, a condition that causes the body to use up energy more quickly than it should, increasing metabolism. An underactive thyroid produces too little thyroid hormone, resulting in hypothyroidism, a condition that causes the body to use energy more slowly than it needs, reducing metabolism.

Parathormone is a hormone produced by the parathyroid glands, usually found in the neck situated on the posterior surface of the thyroid gland. The main function of the parathyroid glands is to maintain calcium levels in the body, so that the nervous and muscular systems can function properly. When blood calcium levels drop below a certain point the parathyroid releases hormone into the blood. The parathyroid hormone also contributes to the control of calcium and phosphorus homeostasis. It also increases gastrointestinal calcium absorption by activating vitamin D, and promotes calcium uptake by the kidneys.

Note:

The above information about hormones is clearly far from complete. What we do know about them is proving to be the tip of the iceberg. New information about hormones and their role in our lives is continually emerging. It is therefore important for students to keep themselves up to date with new developments.

Module 1 – The Chemistry of Stress

Anxiety/Stress

The term anxiety is often used to describe a subjective experience of a state of being that is often expressed emotionally (tears, aggressive and reactive outbursts etc.) but rarely articulated beyond vague generalisations. On the other hand, the term 'worry' can usually be related to a specific issue. Yet the difference between anxiety and worry is only a question of focus. It could be argued that anxiety is a negative anticipation of possible events and worry is a negative anticipation of an expected event or events; the chemistry is the same in either case. Heightened anxiety levels indicate an increase in the activity of the Fight/Flight mechanism. Thus, rumours of imminent redundancies at work may be interpreted as a threat to the security and well-being of our life-style and family, indeed the very thought of the implications may ramp up the activity of the sympathetic nervous system and generate a state of anxiety. When there is no immediate threat to deal with, as may well be the case with rumours, the chemistry of the F/F mechanism (sympathetic nervous system) is given no form of expression that might indicate closure, resulting in a build-up of symptoms (listed below), thus increasing tension and anxiety. This is a major contributor to stress and if prolonged or unresolved will result in a decrease in general performance and a range of debilitating and potentially life-threatening illnesses and diseases.

Physical Symptoms of the F/F Mechanism

1. Hormones such as adrenaline are pumped into the blood
2. Metabolism increases
3. The heartbeat is increased to carry extra oxygen to cells
4. Breathing becomes rapid and shallow
5. The liver releases sugar into the blood
6. Reduction of blood flow to digestive organs, hands and feet
7. Blood flow to the brain and major muscles increased
8. The senses are heightened, particularly the eyes which dilate to allow more light to enter
9. Muscles tense ready for movement
10. Diarrhoea/constipation

Anxiety is therefore a barometer of the activity of the F/F mechanism. It is something we commonly perceive by feeling; how we feel influences what we think, and what we think influences our feelings. Consequently, if the thought is negatively charged, such as the redundancy example given above might be, then the fight/flight mechanism will engage and our feelings will be full of anxiety, which will reinforce our interpretation of the thought itself; thereby establishing a vicious cycle. Recognising this cyclic process is the first step in identifying and thereafter acknowledging anxiety. Once recognised it is possible to modify the cycle, either to take the negative charge out of it or even to give it a positive charge through thinking positively.

Positive Thinking

Our interpretation of an event or a situation will be generally based upon our past experience. Habitually imagining worst-case scenarios induces anxiety states that inevitably lead to stress and the inability to make the most of a situation, because when we are stressed, we not only feel threatened by an event or situation, but we also believe that we are not able to deal with the perceived threat. Thus in many ways history repeats itself.

That every situation has the potential for change is a matter of fact. Yet change does not have to be negative or destructive, we can adapt. Rather than dwelling on the possible negative outcomes of any given situation or event, inviting them to happen as it were, we can develop the habit of seeking and dwelling on the possible positive outcomes of any situation – seeking the good in all things. One method is to imagine different 'good' solutions, looking for the best possible outcome that may arise from any situation, and then, to reflect upon what would be required of us to bring it about. Thus, in the context of any situation we may develop a plan of action that is constructive and beneficial, rather than stewing in a sea of anxiety.

Such 'positive' thinking is not only motivating and empowering; it forms the basis of creative rational thought and a healthy imagination. Imagination is a very powerful tool to which we all have access. It is something we use continually, whether we are conscious of it or not. Imagination is not merely a process of visualisation but an internal form of story telling, a multifaceted form of 'what if'. More often than not we engage in reactive imagining; responding to life's situations according to habit and conditioning. Nevertheless, we can develop our imagination to serve us positively and creatively, thereby enhancing our lives. It is out of such 'positive' thinking that a true 'can do' attitude arises. Yet, no matter how wonderful such benefits might be, the most important benefit is that by using the imagination 'positively' we may usefully affect the underlying biology of the F/F mechanism; particularly when used in conjunction with breath control.

Breath Control

In our society much of our recreational time is devoted to using the sympathetic nervous system, in 'exercise' through sport and athletics as a means of achieving some form of relaxation. It is only natural that we should approach meditation with the same mindset. However, as many people have discovered, when they engage in meditation they quickly find themselves physically uncomfortable and their minds more active than normal; this because they are in a sympathetic nervous system mode, and because we devote so much time to functioning in this mode it should come as no surprise that we know so little about how to achieve an effective level of relaxation.

Rapid/Shallow Breathing

One of the most notable features in the sympathetic nervous system, and of a state of anxiety in general, is rapid and or shallow breathing. In contrast, one of the main characteristics of the parasympathetic nervous system is a slowing down and deepening of the breathing. Alternatively, learning to work with the parasympathetic nervous system, to develop it as a coping mechanism in our everyday activities, should be considered as an evolutionary quantum leap. It is not difficult to engage with. The key to activating it is simply a process of consciously managing one's breathing, learning to slow it down and deepen it, and combining it with the imagination to develop a method of relaxation.

Managing the rate and depth of breathing is a key factor in controlling the autonomic nervous system and the endocrines. There is nothing new in this; breath control has been central to meditation for millennia. The following technique is an old tried-and-tested method for developing and strengthening the parasympathetic nervous system

Brain Wave Patterns

The presence of brain waves was discovered in the early 1920s by a German scientist called Hans Berger. He recognised that the Beta wave registered when mental activity was predominant and the Alpha wave when a state of passivity was predominant. Since his time two more brain wave patterns have been recognised: Theta and Delta. Theta waves register just before sleep and Delta during sleep.

There are four major brain-wave patterns: Beta, Alpha, Theta and Delta. The electrical signals of these brain waves are measured as shown in Fig. 4.

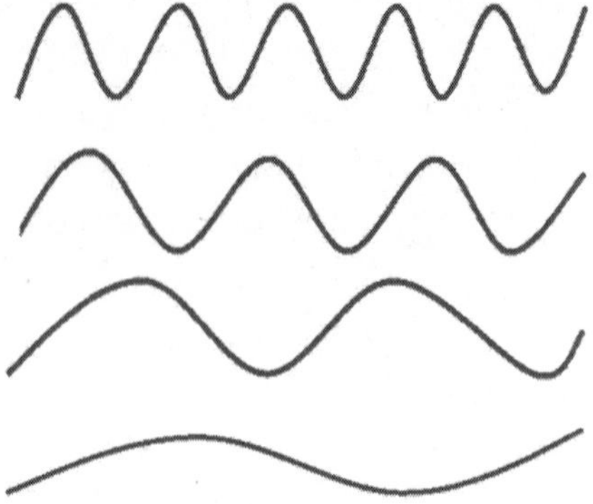

Fig. 4 Brain Waves

Normal consciousness fluctuates between the Beta and Alpha State – between a relatively alert and relaxed state (13 – 15 hertz).

Fig. 5 Normal Beta State

Stress is indicated when our attention is maintained (through worry and anxiety for example) for prolonged periods in the Beta state, particularly at the higher end of its range (20 – 25 hertz).

Fig. 6 Heightened Beta State

The increase in frequency clearly indicates that the body is not functioning within normal levels but in an intensified state of readiness, in anticipation of an imminent emergency action (fight/flight). It is a state that consumes a great deal of the body's resources and will rapidly undermine our ability to function, even under normal circumstances. Alternatively, when our attention is maintained in the alpha state we are likely to fall asleep. However, it must be remembered that there is only one wave vibrating at different frequencies.

Summary

Everyone experiences anxiety, tension and to some degree stress and most of the time it is not a problem and we cope relatively well. The issue we are seeking to address is not that we suffer from stress, although it is a subject worth exploring, rather it is the comprehension of the chemistry of anxiety and stress that must be our objective. It is important to recognise how it influences our consciousness, because only when we can see to what extent it is involved in our lives are we able to begin the process of disentangling the chemist from the chemistry.

Without the understanding that comes with the knowledge of this chemistry all our efforts will be in vain, and the best we can hope to achieve is an endorphin rush – a temporary modification of the chemistry of anxiety – a feel good factor for the moment. Alternatively, it is possible to develop another coping mechanism that is not based upon the dynamic fight/flight mechanism of the sympathetic nervous system but the gentle yet powerful mechanism of the parasympathetic nervous system. It is to this end that the following relaxation exercises are devised.

Module 2 – The Mechanics of Meditation

Relaxation

Because relaxation is the first step towards becoming proficient in meditation it is important that the basic skills of relaxation are mastered, the key to which, especially at the beginning, lies in the regulation of the breath. It is through the breath that effective control can be established over the tensions within both the body and the mind. It is indeed the fulcrum upon which effective meditation rests; hence the beginning of meditation is the beginning of a new attitude to breathing.

Breathing Exercise 1

The purpose of this exercise is to regulate the breathing, and to slow the breathing rate down to about 8 – 10 breaths a minute, thereby promoting parasympathetic nervous system activity.

The success of the relaxation technique outlined below depends upon gentle rhythmic breathing. The method of rhythmic breathing is as follows:

Module 2 – The Mechanics of Meditation

Inhale gently through the nostrils: the breath must be full but not strained

Hold the breath for a moment

Exhale gently through the nostrils, emptying the lungs completely

Hold the breath for a moment

Allow the breath to flow gently and easily – it will soon find its own level – force nothing.

One whole cycle includes: inhale, hold, exhale, hold.

Environment

1. Allow yourself sufficient time free from commitments to engage in this subject without haste.

2. Wear loose comfortable clothing.

3. Choose a place that is clean and free from disturbance i.e. people, telephones, noisy traffic etc.

4. Sit in a firm but comfortable chair, ensuring that the spine is straight and that the head is balanced comfortably, without leaning too far forward or backward.

5. Alternatively, lie down on the floor.

Relaxation Exercise 1

The purpose of this exercise is to develop a physiological mechanism that is linked to the parasympathetic nervous system process.

Step 1

Sit comfortably in a firm but comfortable chair, ensuring that the spine is straight and that the head is balanced comfortably, without leaning too far forward or backward. Commence the above breathing exercise until the breath is flowing gently and easily.

Step 2

Once established, focus your attention upon your feet, tense them, then relax them, and imagine all of the muscles of your feet loosening and becoming limp. Take your time, co-ordinate this, and all subsequent steps, with two or three cycles of the breathing exercise.

Step 3

Focus your attention upon your ankles, tense them, then relax them and imagine the muscles in your ankles loosening and becoming limp.

Step 4

Focus your attention upon your calves, tense them, then relax them and imagine the muscles in your calves loosening and becoming limp.

Step 5

Focus your attention upon your knees and thighs, tense them, then relax them and imagine the muscles in them loosening and becoming limp.

Step 6

Focus your attention upon your lower abdomen, tense the muscles thereabouts, then relax them and imagine all of the muscles therein loosening and becoming limp.

Step 7

Focus your attention upon the muscles around your solar plexus, tense them, then relax them and imagine all of these muscles loosening and becoming limp.

Step 8

Focus your attention upon the muscles of your back, tense them, then relax them and imagine them loosening and becoming limp.

Step 9

Focus your attention upon the muscles of your chest, tense them, then relax them and imagine all of them loosening and becoming limp.

Step 10

Focus your attention upon the muscles of your fingers and arms, tense them, then relax them and imagine all of them loosening and becoming limp.

Step 11

Focus your attention upon the muscles of your neck, tense them, then relax them and imagine all of the muscles of the neck loosening and becoming limp.

Step 12

Focus your attention upon the muscles on and around your head, tense them, then relax them and imagine them loosening and becoming limp.

Step 13

Focus your attention upon the muscles around your eyes, tense them, then relax them and imagine them loosening and becoming limp.

Step 14

Focus your attention on the muscles of your face and jaw, tense them, then relax them and imagine them loosening and becoming limp.

Step 15

Focus your attention on the tongue, tense it, then relax it and imagine it loosening and becoming limp.

Step 16

Now focus your attention upon your whole body, take note of how you feel and observe the influence that the ebb and flow of your breath has upon your overall condition. Allow the rhythm of your breathing to deepen the feeling of relaxation in your muscles.

Used together the above techniques reduce both central nervous system activity and brainwave activity (from Beta to Alpha).

Breathing Exercise 2

This exercise is an extension of the first. It is designed to reduce the breathing rate to approx. 4 breaths per minute and deepen your relaxation.

Inhale gently through the nostrils, whilst mentally counting one thousand, two thousand, three thousand, four thousand.

Hold the breath for about the same length of time as the inhalation whilst mentally counting one thousand, two thousand, three thousand, four thousand.

Exhale gently through the nostrils, emptying the lungs completely whilst mentally counting one thousand, two thousand, three thousand, four thousand.

Hold the breath for about the same length of time as the exhalation whilst mentally counting one thousand, two thousand, three thousand, four thousand.

As in Exercise 1, allow the breath to flow gently and easily – it will soon find its own level – force nothing. One whole cycle includes; inhale, hold, exhale, hold, and takes roughly 16 seconds.

Relaxation Exercise 2

The purpose of this exercise is to reduce muscular tension to the bare minimum.

Step 1

As before, sit comfortably in a firm seat, ensuring that the spine is straight and that the head is balanced comfortably, without leaning too far forward or backward. Commence the above breathing exercise until the breath is flowing gently and easily.

Step 2

Once established, focus your attention upon your feet; on the in-breath focus all of your attention upon your feet and ankles and imagine all the vital energy withdrawing from your feet and ankles into your calves. On the out-breath imagine your feet and ankles letting go of all muscle tone. Do this for three cycles of the breathing exercise.

Step 3

Focus your attention upon your legs; on the in-breath focus all of your attention upon your legs and mentally withdraw all vital energy from them into your lower abdomen. On the out-breath imagine your legs letting go of all muscle tone. Do this for three cycles of the breathing exercise.

Step 4

Focus your attention upon your lower abdomen; on the in-breath mentally withdraw all vital energy from it into your solar plexus. On the out-breath imagine letting go of all muscle tone in your lower abdomen. Do this for three cycles of the breathing exercise.

Step 5

Focus your attention upon the muscles of your back; on the in-breath mentally withdraw all vital energy from them into your solar plexus. On the out-breath imagine letting go of all muscle tone in your back. Do this for three cycles of the breathing exercise.

Step 6

Focus your attention upon the muscles of your hands; on the in-breath mentally withdraw all vital energy from them into your arms. On the out-breath imagine letting go of all muscle tone in your arms. Do this for three cycles of the breathing exercise.

Step 7

Focus your attention upon the muscles of your arms; on the in-breath mentally withdraw all vital energy from them into your solar plexus. On the out-breath imagine letting go of all muscle tone in your arms. Do this for three cycles of the breathing exercise.

Step 8

Focus your attention on the muscles of your face; jaw and tongue, on the in-breath mentally withdraw all vital energy from them into your solar plexus. On the out-breath imagine letting go of all muscle tone in face, jaw and tongue. Do this for three cycles of the breathing exercise.

Step 9

Focus your attention upon the muscles of your neck; on the in-breath mentally withdraw all vital energy from them into your solar plexus. On the out-breath imagine letting go of all muscle tone in your neck. Do this for three cycles of the breathing exercise

Step 10

Now focus your attention upon your whole body; on the in-breath mentally withdraw all vital energy from the body into your solar plexus. On the out-breath imagine letting go of all muscle tone in your body. Do this for three cycles of the breathing exercise. Take note of how you feel and observe the influence that the ebb and flow of your breath has upon your overall condition. Allow the rhythm of your breathing to deepen the feeling of relaxation in your muscles. Allow any everyday worry or concern that you may have to fade away with exhalation of your breath. Imagine them dissipating as your relaxation deepens – enjoy the experience.

• • •

When the two exercises above are combined effectively, they bring about a profound state of relaxation (reducing the brainwave frequency from Alpha to Theta). THEREFORE; THIS EXERCISE SHOULD NOT EXCEED 15 MINUTES' DURATION. After a few minutes spent practising this exercise you should allow your breathing to find its own level and rate!

Notes

All of the foregoing exercises are relaxation exercises only; they are not in themselves meditation. They can and should be developed as skill that may be used as life-skills in general.

Neck

When working with Relaxation Exercise 1 (step 11) take a little time to stretch the neck by putting your chin on your chest and tipping the head forward.

Eyes & Vision

Normal vision is object-focussed. This means that we 'see', more often than not, by focussing our attention on an object; our eyes skip from one object to another. If we are in a tricky situation we tend to concentrate our vision on the area that is giving us the problem. However, when we close our eyes, in bed for instance, our eyes normally go out of focus and we drift into sleep. This mechanism acts as a switch or trigger to activate the parasympathetic nervous system, so when we relax our eyes by defocussing them we increase our ability to relax considerably.

It is a simple exercise. First, place the forefinger of each hand about six inches in front of your eyes. Now move the fingers away from the centre and around your head towards the ears. There is a point where the finger disappears from sight; this is the perimeter or periphery of your field of vision. Now close your eyes and do not focus on anything. Second, examine your field of vision from the perimeters, observe everything simultaneously; look at the field not at what's in or on it. You can do this with your eyes open or closed. It is a technique that has been utilised in various disciplines for generations.

Tongue & Jaw

Speech is the main organ of communication. The tongue and jaw are ever ready for action, thus it should come as no surprise that they have a direct relationship to the sympathetic nervous system. Consciously relaxing them releases the tension contained in the jaw like the energy in a coiled spring and will greatly benefit the relaxation process.

Hands & Fingers

Like the tongue and jaw, the hands are directly influenced by the sympathetic nervous system. They are the power-tools that we use to modify our environment, and like the tongue and jaw they can be reservoirs of a great deal of tension. (Try and relax whilst maintaining clenched fists.) Consciously relaxing the hands, finger by finger, releases tension throughout the body, thereby improving the relaxation process.

Module 3 – Concentrating the Mind

Visualisation

The purpose of the following exercises is to identify and develop the image-making faculty. From a practical perspective, it must be assumed that the student has no image-making ability.

All of the following exercises are designed to be cultivated in the relaxed state outlined in Module 2. Work with one exercise per session.

Geometric Forms

Imagine a tiny dot of light in space. Imagine this dot expanding until it forms a large circle. Now imagine this circle as a sphere; explore it.

Imagine a tiny dot of light in space oscillating up and down, forming a line. Imagine this line spinning on a central axis forming a circle. Imagine this circle stabilising; explore it.

Find any spherical object, study it, and then create a mental image of it. Explore this image with the mind's eye, looking at it from every angle (this makes particular sense if the object has a design on it).

Module 3 – Concentrating the Mind

Find or make:

A three-dimensional triangle (a tetrahedron); study it, then make a mental image of it. Explore the geometry of the image with the mind's eye, looking at it from every angle.

A small cube; study it, then create a mental image of it. Explore the geometry of this image with the mind's eye, looking at it from every angle. (This includes looking at it from within.)

Natural Forms

Acquire a simple natural form such as a leaf or a stone; gaze at it steadily, explore its shape, its colour, its size, its feel, smell etc. After you have explored it sufficiently, close your eyes and imagine it; open your eyes again, and compare the mental impression with the physical object. This exercise is well worth repeating several times a day for a week or two, using different forms to develop the image-making faculty.

Select a number of simple natural objects and study them, then imagine each object whilst looking at a blank sheet of paper, then take a pencil and draw each object in turn. As before compare with the originals.

Select an object with texture, explore it, and then create a mental image or impression of it. As before compare with the original.

Using any musical instrument, strike a note, explore it until satisfied, then form a mental image or impression of the note, then strike it again and compare the note with your impression or image.

Choose something with a specific odour, explore it, then form a mental impression of the odour. Return to the original and compare with your impression.

Select a verse from a poem or a short paragraph from a book. Memorise the selected text and reflect upon it. Note what images and other sensory impressions emerge into your field of awareness.

Manufactured Forms

Acquire any simple manufactured object and study it as described above. Close your eyes and imagine it, explore its underlying geometry, and where feasible see the natural form that may have been the inspiration for its design. Open your eyes and compare your mental impression with the physical object.

Memory

The purpose of the following exercises is to develop the faculty of recall, of remembering past experiences. Work with one exercise per session.

Module 3 – Concentrating the Mind

People

Think of:
Someone you know, imagine him/her standing or sitting before you. Examine the form, the colour of hair, eyes, skin tone, clothing, gestures etc. Look at it from different viewpoints.

Two or more people that you know. Imagine them standing or sitting before you. Explore their forms and (however trivial they may seem) note the differences.

Someone you don't know but may have encountered within the past 24 hours, perhaps on a bus, at work or in a shop. Imagine them standing or sitting before you. Explore the image and note the thoughts and speculations that emerge.

Places

Think of:
A particular interior that you like, it may be your favourite room, or a place you have visited, perhaps whilst on holiday. Imagine that place and explore it with your mind's eye. Note the underlying geometry, the colours, the objects involved and their significance. Explore the site from different angles.

A rural spot that you like. It may be a quiet beach or forest glade or a panoramic viewpoint. Imagine that place and explore it with your mind's eye. Look at it from different viewpoints noting the aspects that make it interesting.

A civic scene that is reasonably well known to you. It may be a classic piece of architecture, a statue, an old village high street or village green. It might even be a busy street or motorway. As before, imagine that place and explore it with your mind's eye, noting the things that make it unique. Again, explore it from different angles.

Events

Think of:
A happy event that is personal to yourself. Recall that event, what it was about and why you were happy. Imagine the location and who if any was present. Note the differences in those present, their mood, attitude, clothing, what they were doing etc. Explore the event, look at it from different angles and reflect on why it was so meaningful.

A seasonal event that you experienced, a warm spring picnic, a balmy summer sunset, a walk in the woods on a crisp autumn day or perhaps the first snowfall of winter. Recall the event; imagine the location, and who was present. Explore this event and look at it from different angles and reflect on your experience of it.

A social or national event that has meaning for you. Perhaps it was the collapse of the Berlin Wall, a sports triumph or maybe a great party. Recall the event, imagine the location and who was present. Explore this event and look at it from different angles reflecting on why it was so significant.

Module 3 – Concentrating the Mind

Conceptualisation

The purpose of the following exercises is to identify and develop the thinking faculty, not analyse what we think. Work with one exercise per session. For many students the ability to comprehend an idea (archetype) in the raw is initially beyond their grasp. Often the comprehension of the 'Idea' comes in the later stages of 'concept' or 'proposition'.

Idea

Archetype or pattern as distinguished from its manifest form. (An idea represents the universal nature of a thing stripped of all individuating notes.)

e.g. A drinking vessel
A cutting tool

Concept

A notion concerning an idea, (a representation through which we are able to know an object).

e.g. A cup is a drinking vessel
A knife is a cutting tool

Proposition

A proposal or an assertion: in logic a proposition:

e.g. A small cup made of bone china is a teacup
A knife is a small cutting instrument

Notes on Meditation

Projection

There are many systems that may be used effectively in the following exercise. However, be mindful that the Tradition has its own system.

Objectives

Establishing a clear intention.

- Desire (What do I want?)
- Motive (Why do I want?)
- Purpose (How do I achieve it?)

Modelling

Developing a conceptual representation of objective.
Defining:

- Purpose
- Function
- Design
- Material requirements

Planning

The process of giving the conceptual representation a form

- Priorities [needs analysis]
- Models [defining relationships, what it might look like]
- Mind maps [exploring connections and problem solving]

Brainstorming & Mind Maps

Brainstorming and mind maps are valuable tools for organising thoughts and ideas. Used in conjunction or individually they are very useful for making sense out of what may appear at first to be disparate and or disjointed impressions acquired in our meditations. They can also provide a means of selecting and ordering initial ideas from the dense and inscrutable texts that from time to time form the subject matter of our meditations.

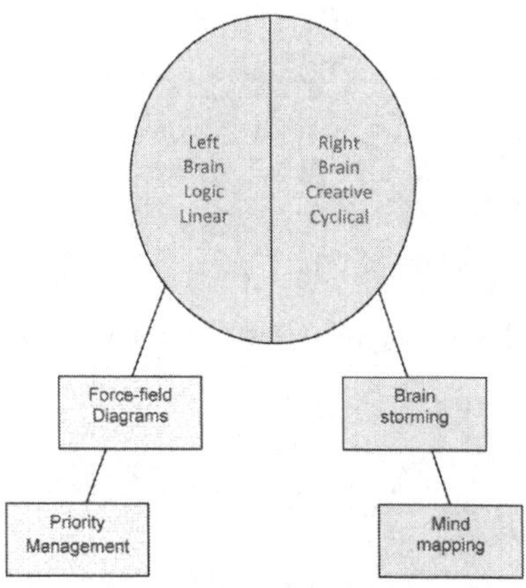

Fig. 7 Left & Right Brain Modes

Fig. 7 outlines what is embodied in this module. It alludes to a world of human endeavour that has many disciplines and many skilled exponents, particularly in the realms of education and business. It is easy to lose yourself in this area as there are many enticing avenues full of interest, with many tools to play with; a few of which are used in this module. However, although limited, what follows is sufficient for the purpose of enabling effective meditation.

Force-field analysis outlines the positive [pros] and negative [cons] elements of an issue.

The issue...!
+ Positive (pro's)
- Negative (cons)

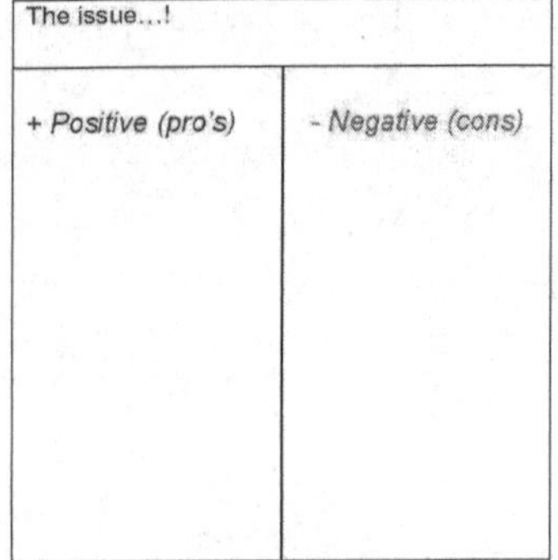

Fig. 8 Force-field Analysis

Priority Management Matrix

[A useful tool, first popularised by Stephen Covey[1], for prioritising needs and allocating time according to need.]

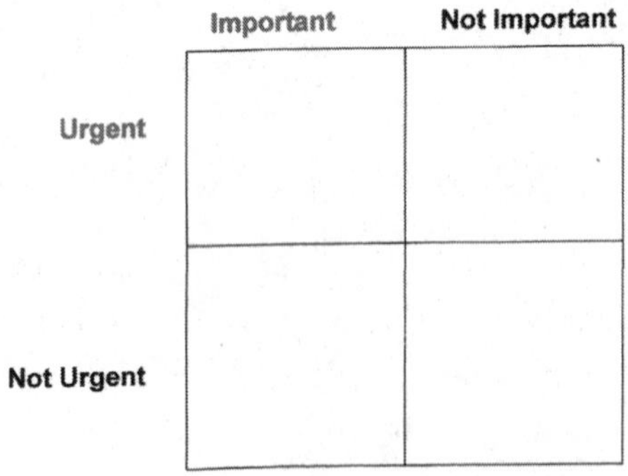

Important
Not Important
Urgent
Not Urgent

Fig. 9 Priority Management Matrix

---

1 *Seven Habits of Highly Effective People*, Stephen Covey, Freepress, London, 1989.

Brainstorming

Brainstorming is a 'free-association' method of exploring an idea or discovering a solution to a problem. It works by focussing on the idea or problem, and then deliberately coming up with as many connections or solutions as possible (plausible or otherwise) and by exploring all ideas that emerge as far as one can.

Although brainstorming may appear at first to be alien to the spirit of meditation the principles of this exercise may be quickly assimilated and employed as an interior process of exploring ideas, especially ideas that have emerged in the form of inspiration. Such an occurence is not infrequent; many students have inspired insights during meditation, even though many lose sight of them or are unable to recall the nature of what took place.

During a brainstorming session (especially a group session) there must be no criticism of any thoughts and ideas that might arise, as every idea is open to as many possibilities as the imagination can muster. However, brainstorming is not simply a random activity. It needs to be structured and should follow a few simple rules. A generic process is outlined below:

1. Define (and agree) the objective
2. Establish a time limit to the exercise
3. Brainstorm ideas
4. Sort the information (e.g. mind mapping)

5. Assess the results (e.g. force-field analysis)
6. Prioritise the results (priority management matrix)
7. Formulate next step

Allocate a time limit and keep the objective simple, ensuring that everyone participating understands and agrees the aim of the session. This will enable you to keep the random nature of brainstorming under control.

You will need a flip-chart or whiteboard, or some other means of recording information. This is important because brainstorming usually involves an outpouring of information that may not be obviously connected to the problem, and if it is a group activity then everyone must be able to see what is emerging. Use the tools described in Module 3, and any other tools that you find useful, such as a notebook to record the results of your endeavours.

Mind Maps

Mind mapping is a means by which we may visually represent our thoughts and ideas. It is also a means of collating the brainstorming 'free-association' process. As such it can be an invaluable aid to effective meditation because it is essentially a graphic technique enabling us to construct a visual representation of our thoughts and deliberations about a given subject – enabling us to establish a formal structure to interconnected thoughts.

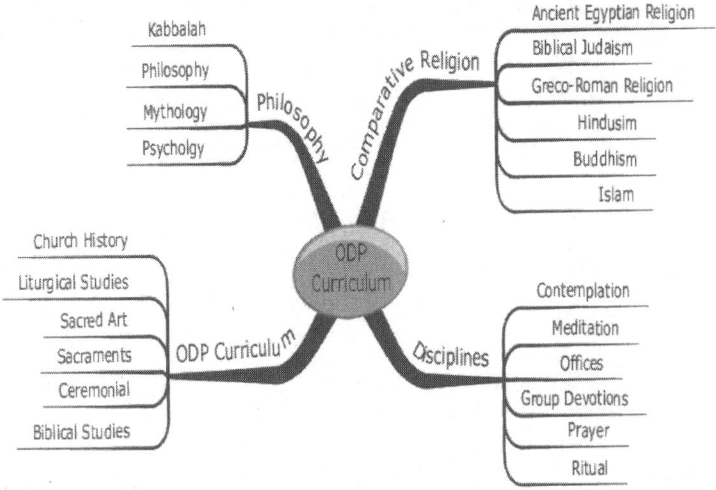

Fig. 10 ODP Curriculum Mind Map

Mind maps are simple to use and very effective tools for arranging and making sense of the data that emerges from a brainstorming session. Creating a mind map usually requires that we focus upon a central principle or idea from which all possible connections are drawn. For example, the mind map illustrated above gives a graphic representation of the Order of Dionysis and Paul Curriculum, which clearly illustrates four main areas of study and activity.

It should be noted that each of the sub-headings stemming from the four main branches illustrated in Fig. 10 could easily be expanded into many sub-branches, as it is obvious that each sub-heading is in itself an area capable of being divided into many sectors of study and research. The potential is limited only by the imagination and understanding of the student. Often the creation of such a mind map is the consolidation of emerging ideas and may be the beginning of a lengthy and fruitful course of study that may take years to complete. During this time, the general shape of the map will expand and evolve as the study progresses.

A mind map has four essential characteristics:

1. The core subject is crystallised in a central image/notion.

2. Themes derived from the core subject radiate from it as the main connecting branches.

3. Topics of lesser significance are represented as secondary branches deriving from the main connecting branches.

4. The branches form an interlinked nodal structure with the core subject forming a central axis connecting all of the main themes.

Mind mapping enables the student to arrange thoughts and ideas into a simple form, which when complete will serve as a visual aid giving a clear visual representation of what may seem at first to be a complex muddle of thought. For this reason alone developing the simple skills involved in mind mapping (following the four steps above) is well worth the time and effort involved.

As a point of interest it is worth noting that a great deal of the sacred art produced by many cultures may be considered as an exercise in mind mapping, where symbols have been used to represent key ideas instead of words.

Module 4 – Controlled Imagining

Having first established a solid foundation for meditation by developing the relaxation and concentration exercises outlined in Modules 1 to 3, it is now time to begin meditation. The oldest and simplest form of meditation consists in establishing a profound state of relaxation in which the attention is focused upon a given point such as the breath as it passes in and out of the nostrils.

Inevitably, it will not be long before the attention is led away from the breath by a procession of thoughts, images and sensations entering into the field of awareness, clamouring for attention. This unruly behaviour is common, normal, predictable and well documented. However, remembering that self-knowledge is a key feature of meditation, it is of far greater value looking at the nature of those intrusive thoughts, images and sensations than rejecting or suppressing them. This is because the quickest way of overcoming them is through understanding them, whereas rejecting or suppressing them will turn them into insurmountable obstacles that will bar any progress until dealt with appropriately. Their presence is both a sign that you are on the right path and a challenge to your entrenched egocentricity.

Although an important objective of meditation is self-knowledge, in traditional terms the ultimate objective is a detachment from all activity that we may enter into the exalted state of contemplation. This state is a natural evolution of the regular practice of meditation, a movement beginning with the activity of using the faculties of the mind culminating in non-activity and entering the 'silence'. However, it is true to say that this state may may take a considerable time to achieve.

One of the early fruits of meditation is a greater understanding of the chemistry of consciousness and the nature of experience through what is best described as 'insight'. 'Insight' is a term that describes one's ability to acquire a profound understanding of an object through the sustained concentration of the attention upon it. It is a faculty that lies beyond rational thought, indeed it is more of the nature of intuition or gnosis and it enables us to enter the hidden depths of the field of experience and understand its effect upon our consciousness. This does not require us to examine every thought, image or feeling individually; that would be a never-ending and foolish path to follow. No, it means that by observing the field of our experience we learn something of its true immaterial nature, and also, to distinguish the knower from the field of knowledge – which is the first great task of the spiritual alchemist! The following exercises are designed with this objective in mind.

Exercise 1 – Reflections on the Body I

Follow the relaxation procedure (Module 2); begin the breathing exercise until the breath is flowing gently and easily. Once established, concentrate your attention upon the physical body. Just as in the concentration exercises, explore the body, note everything. Ask yourself, is it merely an amorphous lump of conflicting sensations or is there more to it? What is it, and what do we know about it? What are its constituent parts? You might think it consists of cells; ask yourself then, what is a cell, what do cells do, how do they organise themselves? You might think that they organise themselves into systems; if that be true then what systems? Consider the following and meditate on their individual significance:

Skeletal system

Muscular system

Nervous system

Lymphatic system

Digestive system

Respiratory system

Endocrine system

Cardio-vascular system

Reproductive system

Renal System

Immune system

The Cell

This extraordinary micro-system is the basic building block of all of the aforementioned systems, indeed, of all life forms. The cell is a completely self-contained system separated from its environment by a selectively permeable membrane that consists of layers of phospholipids and proteins. It is selectively permeable to certain ions and organic molecules thereby controlling the movement of material in and out of the cell. The cell-membrane also controls the electric potential of the cell, indeed according to Georges Lakhosky[1] (1869 – 1942), a Russian biologist and engineer, cells are electrical units whose underlying mechanism is the oscillating circuit from which energy is given off in the form of waves.

The interior of the cell is filled with a jelly-like substance called cytoplasm. The cell also contains its own micro-organs called organelles that function in relation to the cell in much the same manner as organs to the body. These organelles are also enclosed within their own membranes, suggesting a similar function to the cell-membrane itself. The largest of them is the nucleus, which is the control centre of the cell, within which is to be found DNA – the basic material of our genes – and RNA, which contains the coding for constructing substances such as amino acids and enzymes. For many health professionals the health of the cell is considered to be fundamental to maintaining the health of the body.

---

1 *The Secret of Life*, Georges Lakhovsky, William Heinemann, London, 1939.

Module 4 – Controlled Imagining

Exercise 2 – Reflections on the Body II

Consider the body in terms of the following: matter, form, energy. Thus:

Matter
What do we mean by the term 'matter'?
Is the matter of the body all the same?
What effect has matter upon Self?

Form
What do we mean by the term 'form'?
What are the different forms of the body?
What influence do these different forms
have upon the Self?

Energy
What do we mean by the term 'energy'?
Where does this energy come from?
What part does this energy play in the body?
What influence does it have upon the Self?

What is Self? .....?

It is possible to consider this question from a:

Materialistic/mechanistic perspective
Psychological perspective
Spiritual perspective

Notes on Meditation

There are many views and opinions about the nature of the 'Self' and many of them are worth exploring, but the most import point is to arrive at a personal understanding, no matter how limited it might be. It matters little if you consider your views naïve or of no consequence, it is where you start from that is important, whereas starting from someone else's understanding will only serve to confuse. Furthermore, it does not have to be shared with others. Therefore, arriving at a point where you have your own definition is important as it establishes a platform to operate from, a platform that will enable you to develop your own understanding.

Record your reflections in a notebook, it will be invaluable as you progress.

Module 4 – Controlled Imagining

Exercise 3 – The Sphere of Sensation

The main vehicles of human experience in the physical world are the sensory organs of the physical body. All experience gained thereby is invariably conditioned by the biological changes taking place in the world moment by moment, nano-second by nano-second. Therefore, some recognition and understanding of that biology is essential if the student is to make progress. The body is not just a solid mass of flesh – a vehicle of physical sensation only – no matter how much we are accustomed to think of it as such. It is a beautiful world of integrated systems that are exquisitely complex and worthy of the greatest respect, and a close examination of it will reveal this microcosmic world to be a perfect reflection of the macrocosm.

Traditionally, the body was viewed as a synthesis of the four elements – earth, air, fire and water – and from our perspective this model is still fit for purpose. Earth corresponds with matter in a solid state, water with matter in a liquid state, air with matter in a gaseous state and fire with pure energy. Thus, earth corresponds with the physical aspects of our body, the skeleton being the most obvious, but also includes the brain, the central nervous system, muscles, cartilage and tendons etc.

Water corresponds with the fluidic parts of our body, particularly the blood and the lymph, air with the pulmonary system centred in the lungs, and fire with the nervous energy flowing through the nervous system. This model is extremely useful to begin with, as it opens up the dark continent of our physical body to observation. However, although it provides a good overview a more detailed model will provide us with a greater understanding, and it was with this purpose in mind that Exercise 1 on page 70 was given. It is an exercise worth persevering with.

With regards to the sphere of sensation, we are informed that it is an egg-shaped sphere of electro-magnetic energy that surrounds and contains the human body and that it is generated from within the body in much the same way as the Earth's magnetic field is thought to be generated in and by the Earth's core, and as far as we know serves a similar purpose. This field or sphere of sensation is understood to be a vessel which receives the influx of the Divine Light analogous to the way the atmosphere of our planet receives photons of light from the Sun, and as such constitutes the foundation of all living things on Earth. It is possible to see in the structure of this mechanism an analogue of the electro-magnetic structure and activity of both the cell and the solar system, which suggests an archetypal model applying to all living things, at least in our world.

The substance contained within the sphere of sensation is extremely fluid and generally in constant motion; indeed, throughout history it has often been alluded to as a sea or an ocean with its own tides and currents. However, the water referred to here is not H_2O but a body of energy with the fluidic qualities of water, and a major part of the student's work lies in understanding and rising above the influences and effects of the forces manifesting within this body of energy.

Module 4 – Controlled Imagining

The forces operating within the sphere of sensation, like the ocean itself, are never still; sometimes they are very unstable and have frequently been described in metaphorical terms as storms and tempests. This is particularly significant because in meditation one of the major problems to confront students, particularly at the beginning, is the constant bombardment of thoughts, feelings and images dancing before the mind's eye. Few perceive this chemistry as an activity of the sphere of sensation; indeed, most simply accept it as the activity of a restless mind in which thoughts and feelings are never still. Others think it evidence that they are incapable of meditating, or perhaps not ready for it. The truth is that this mental noise is merely a part of the chemistry of consciousness taking place within the sphere of sensation, which is simply being true to its nature. It is a chemistry that is shaped and conditioned by the biological programming of the body as it seeks to survive in this world, and it must be understood rather than suppressed.

This biological programming is an expression of a singular primal urge or instinct 'to be', which may be further considered as being expressed in the form of two secondary instincts, 'reproduction' and 'survival'. These instincts are so powerful that the majority of people will go through their entire lives devoted to fulfilling them and nothing else, and rarely, if ever, perceiving the biological imperatives driving them. Almost all of us unconsciously build our identity in the context of these imperatives, which is remarkable because they play a fundamental role in almost every part of our lives. Indeed, they generally determine most of our everyday thinking, particularly in the way we establish our lives around the complex relationships formed within our community and the world at large. For instance, we aspire to a place and a status in the community that will provide us with sufficient personal respect, money and material resources to attract a mate and provide for a family. In our highly mechanised world this means a career that will fund a mortgage and give us sufficient resources to maintain a family and afford a life-style. To achieve this requires an appropriate education, not only in academic studies but also in relationship skills; all of which are set in the context of a community of people by and large striving for the same objectives. For most of us family and career constitute our life.

In human terms this world is the mundane world and we identify the most personal and intimate part of ourselves with this world, invariably failing to recognise that our thoughts and feelings are products of biological drivers interacting with our social environment. Yet, although our thoughts and feelings are predominantly determined by our biology and the environment we live in, our ability to think is essentially a function of the soul, as is the mechanism of thought. Thus, our rational, imaginative and emotional faculties are faculties of our soul and should be acknowledged as such.

Traditionally, the means by which the student is enabled to rise above this biological conditioning is through self-observation, which is to say, that through process of inner reflection it is possible to transcend the flow of transient thought-forms dancing in the light of consciousness and behold the permanent reality that is the substrate of our being and the true ground of the soul, and meditation is the tool designed for such work.

Meditation was designed in the precincts of the sanctuary by the exponents of the spiritual life who understood it to be the first step on the path of self-knowledge. However, as stated earlier, successfully engaging in the work of meditation requires some understanding of the chemistry of consciousness and its environment, and a key part of that environment is the sphere of sensation and the movement of energy continually taking place therein. It is an energy that is linked into the tidal movements of energy of this world and all of the life-forms manifesting within it. That is to say, its movements correspond with the movements of energy in nature. The sphere of sensation is in effect if not in fact a microcosm of the world of nature.

Before one can effectively control the chemistry of consciousness taking place within the sphere of sensation it is necessary to recognise and understand the cyclic movements, or tides as they are sometimes called, of the sphere itself. The movements of energy taking place within the sphere correspond with the changes taking place moment by moment in the macrocosm. One example of such a tide is the circadian cycle. The word 'circadian' derives from the Latin words *circas* and *dies*, meaning *around* and *day*. Thus, the circadian cycle is approximately 24 hours long and a great deal of the natural world is governed by it. In human terms there are several key biochemical processes and activities including physical, mental and behavioural patterns based upon this cycle. Many of these processes respond primarily to light and darkness but can also be affected by other influences. The main biological mechanism that controls the circadian rhythms is located in the hypothalamus gland situated in the brain (see Fig. 3, Endocrinal Glands).

The Sun, which clearly governs the flow of our vital energy, plays a central role in the circadian cycle. Thus, along with many other creatures that rise with the Sun, we are most active in the morning. As the day progresses through the afternoon we gradually become less active, until in the evening, with the setting of the Sun or shortly after, we naturally drift into sleep. This daily cycle is also reflected on a larger scale in the procession of the seasons where a great outpouring of energy and activity occurs in the natural world during spring and summer, gradually declining into rest during autumn and entering a dormant period akin to sleep during winter.

The energy of the Sun also powers ocean currents and the circulation of the atmosphere. It is the major controlling influence of the Earth's climate and of the human condition. For instance, the lack of sunlight can affect the circadian rhythms disrupting sleep patterns, blood pressure and hormonal activity, thus affecting emotional tides and our ability to act rationally. This can particularly affect those who live at latitudes above 37 degrees north or below 37 degrees south of the equator, where for six months of the year (autumn & winter) exposure to sunlight is much reduced causing health problems for many people. Seasonal affective disorder (SAD) is one such condition that is directly associated with sunlight deprivation.

In conjunction with the Sun, the gravitational impact of the Moon influences the fluidic elements of the Earth – the oceans and seas – causing them to rise and fall twice daily as the Earth turns upon its axis, and has a corresponding influence upon the fluids of our body, especially the blood and lymph. From a human perspective this influence is most noticeable at key times in the cycle of the seasons such as the equinoxes and solstices, and during its 28 day circuit of the Earth, concerning which a great deal of folklore testifies.

Variations in the ionisation of the atmosphere caused by magnetic disturbances such as those produced by the cyclic ebb and flow of solar flares and sunspot activity are now understood to have a direct influence on the metabolism of the body. This phenomenon is also observable on a regional or local level where positive ions at the leading edge of a weather system make us irritable, whilst negative ions, in abundance at the end of a storm, induce a sense of relief and well-being. There are also certain types of winds, such as the Sirocco in Italy or the Autan in France, that bring with them high levels of positive ions. These winds are well known for their disruptive effect on the health and social behaviour of people. Knowledge of the cycles and tides of such forces enable students to arrive at more informed conclusions about the chemistry taking place within their own spheres of sensation.

There are many other examples of rhythmic cycles or tides that are worth exploring, and many of them are very complex, but in truth although controlling them as external forces may be difficult if not impossible, controlling their effects within our own sphere of sensation is not so difficult as one might at first imagine. Control is best effected by harnessing the faculties of imagination and thought, as already discussed (see Module 2) to the rhythmic flow of the breath.

The exercises in Figs 11 to 15 are designed to do just that, with the added benefit of developing the student's ability to stabilise, direct and use the energy flowing in the sphere of sensation thereby improving the quality and nature of the meditation.

Module 4 – Controlled Imagining

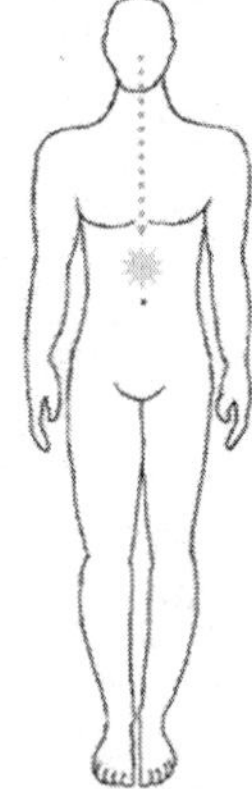

Step 1
Using the four-second breath, breathe in imagining the breath as light flowing into the solar plexus.

Hold

Step 2
Breathe out, imagining the breath as light flowing from the solar plexus, up through the chest, over the shoulders, along the arms and out through the hands, extending beyond them for approximately 5cm.

Hold

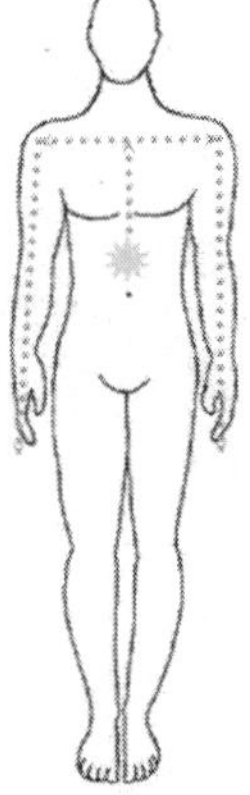

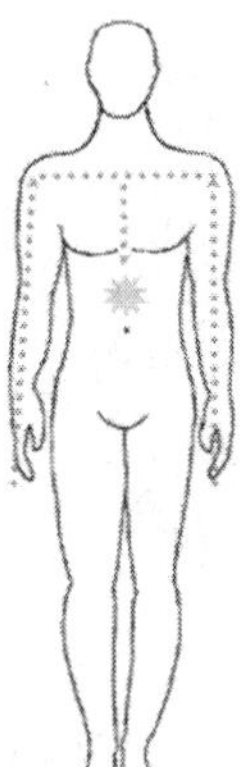

Step 3
Breathe in, imagining the breath as light flowing back through the hands, along the arms and shoulders back into the solar plexus.

Hold

Step 4
You have now completed the upper cycle.

Repeat this cycle 3 – 4 times in succession, morning, noon & evening.

Do not exceed this recommendation!

Fig. 11 Exercise 1

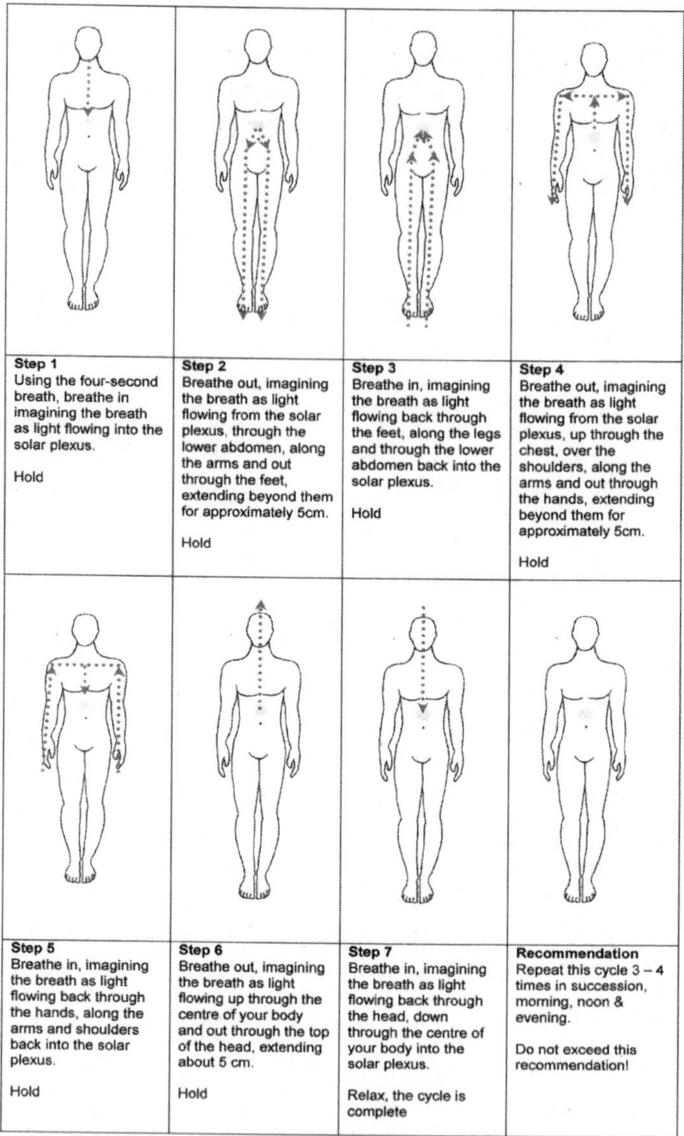

Step 1	Step 2	Step 3	Step 4
Using the four-second breath, breathe in imagining the breath as light flowing into the solar plexus. Hold	Breathe out, imagining the breath as light flowing from the solar plexus, through the lower abdomen, along the arms and out through the feet, extending beyond them for approximately 5cm. Hold	Breathe in, imagining the breath as light flowing back through the feet, along the legs and through the lower abdomen back into the solar plexus. Hold	Breathe out, imagining the breath as light flowing from the solar plexus, up through the chest, over the shoulders, along the arms and out through the hands, extending beyond them for approximately 5cm. Hold

Step 5	Step 6	Step 7	Recommendation
Breathe in, imagining the breath as light flowing back through the hands, along the arms and shoulders back into the solar plexus. Hold	Breathe out, imagining the breath as light flowing up through the centre of your body and out through the top of the head, extending about 5 cm. Hold	Breathe in, imagining the breath as light flowing back through the head, down through the centre of your body into the solar plexus. Relax, the cycle is complete	Repeat this cycle 3 – 4 times in succession, morning, noon & evening. Do not exceed this recommendation!

Fig. 12 Exercise 2

Module 4 – Controlled Imagining

Step 1
Using the four-second breath, breathe in imagining the breath as light flowing into the solar plexus.

Hold

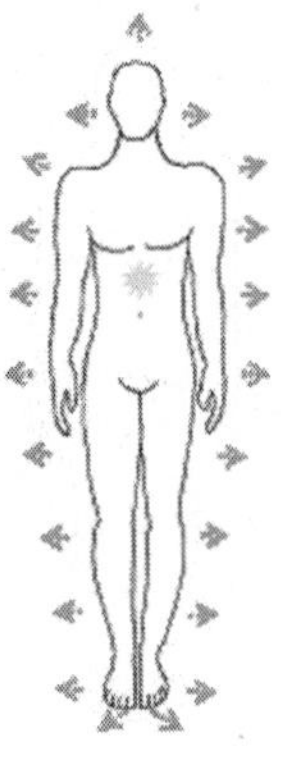

Step 2
Breathe out, imagining the breath as light flowing from the solar plexus, out through the skin, extending beyond the skin for approximately 5cm.

Hold

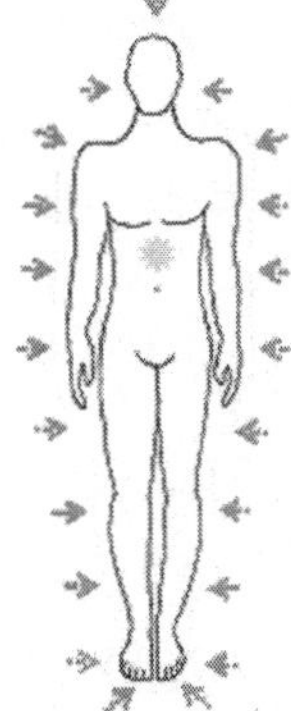

Step 3
Breathe in, imagining the breath as light flowing back through the skin into the solar plexus.

Hold

Step 4
Relax; you have now completed the cycle.

Repeat this cycle 3 – 4 times in succession, morning, noon & evening.

Do not exceed this recommendation!

Fig. 13 Exercise 3

Notes on Meditation

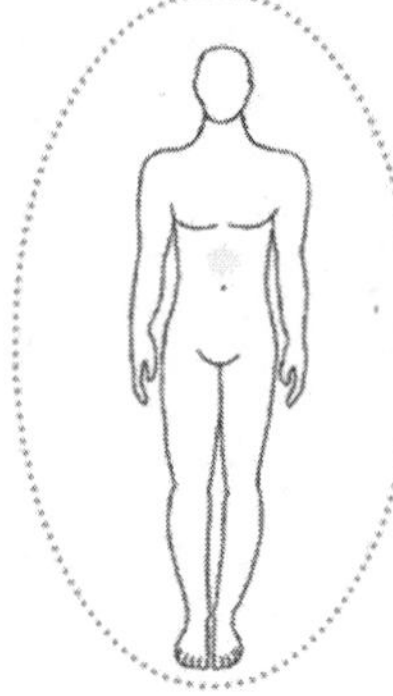

Step 1
Imagine you are standing in an egg of light, with the solar plexus as its centre and source, and the perimeter being about a foot or so away from the body.

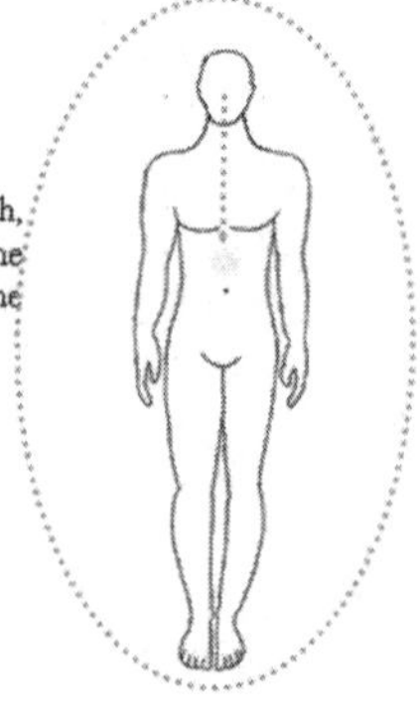

Step 2
Using the four-second breath, breathe in imagining the breath as light flowing into the solar plexus.

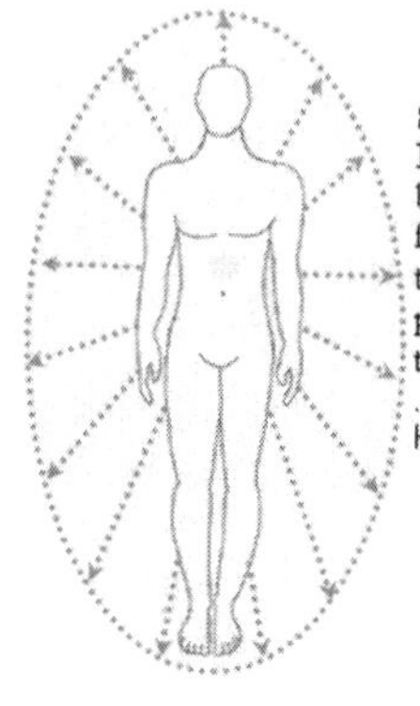

Step 3
Breathe out, imagining the breath as light flowing out from the solar plexus, out through the body to the perimeter of the Egg. Imagine the egg filling with light

Hold

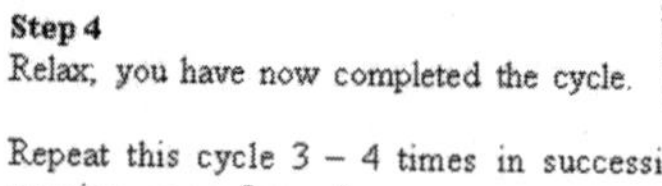

Step 4
Relax; you have now completed the cycle.

Repeat this cycle 3 – 4 times in succession, morning, noon & evening.

Do not exceed this recommendation!

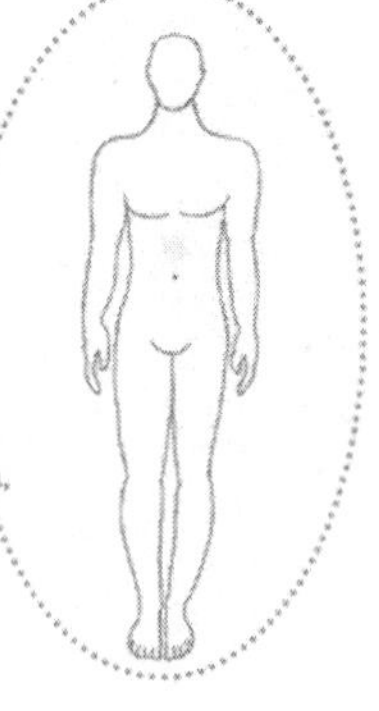

Fig. 14 Exercise 4

Module 4 – Controlled Imagining

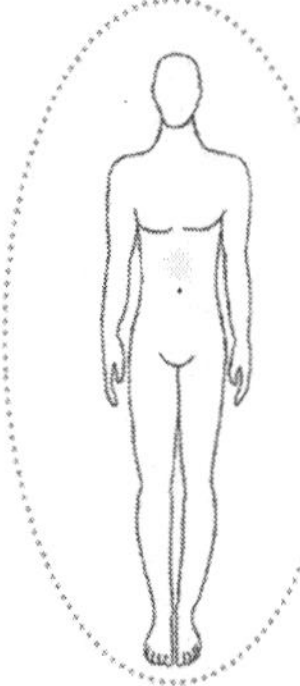

Step 1
Imagine you are standing in an egg of light, with the solar plexus as its centre and source, and the perimeter being about a foot or so away from the body.

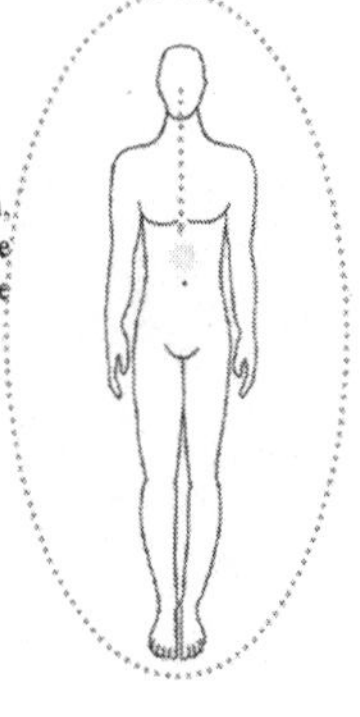

Step 2
Using the four-second breath, breathe in, imagining the breath as light flowing into the solar plexus.

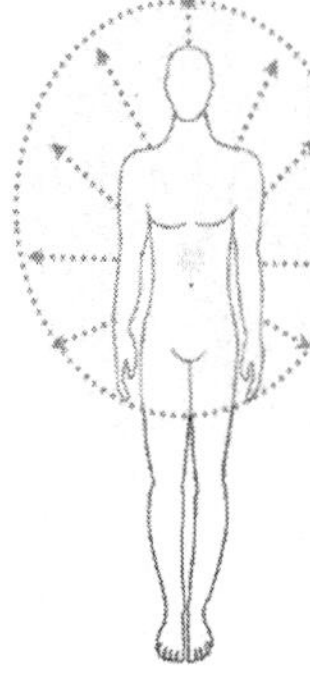

Step 3
Breathe out, imagining the breath as light flowing out from the solar plexus, out through the body to the perimeter of a sphere, thus: Imagine the sphere filling with light.

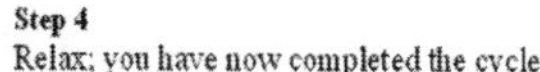

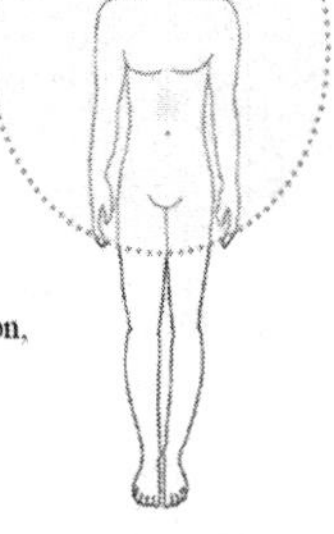

Step 4
Relax; you have now completed the cycle.

Repeat this cycle 3 – 4 times in succession, morning, noon & evening.

Do not exceed this recommendation!

Fig. 15 Exercise 5

Exercise 4 – Reflection on the Day's Events

Follow the relaxation procedure; begin the breathing exercise until the breath is flowing gently and easily. Once established, concentrate your attention upon the day's events, scan through the day noting the activities that were significant.

First, note those events where you may not have behaved in an appropriate manner.

Second, examine each event, asking yourself what you might have done that might have been more appropriate. Replay the scene, modifying your behaviour.

Third, examine each event; think about what other/s might have done that might have been more appropriate. Replay the scene, modifying their behaviour.

Fourth, establish, as far as you possibly can, what it was about the event that you could not have changed.

Fifth, note those events where you behaved in an appropriate manner and explore.

Sixth, note how you feel about the day – are you tired, frustrated, happy etc.

Record your impressions and thoughts in a notebook, it will be invaluable as time progresses.

Module 4 – Controlled Imagining

Exercise 5 – Transient Self I

That we are driven and conditioned by the chemistry of the body and its environment suggests that as the physical and environmental conditions change so will we. The main purpose of this exercise is to recognise the external influences that determine our state of being. Therefore, the main components of the exercise will consist of:

Focusing upon distinguishing between our external sensory awareness and our internal chemistry of consciousness.

Noting the variations in the above and how our personality and disposition varies in relationship to our daily experience.

This exercise should be undertaken daily for at least one month.

Use your notebook to record the results and impression of this exercise.

Procedure

1. Preparation (as described in Module 2 - The Mechanics of Meditation).

2. Allow yourself sufficient time free from commitments to engage in this subject without haste (15 – 30mins).

3. Wear loose comfortable clothing (if possible).

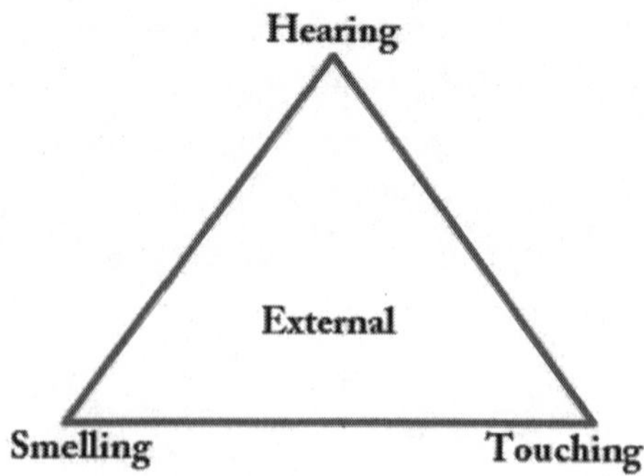

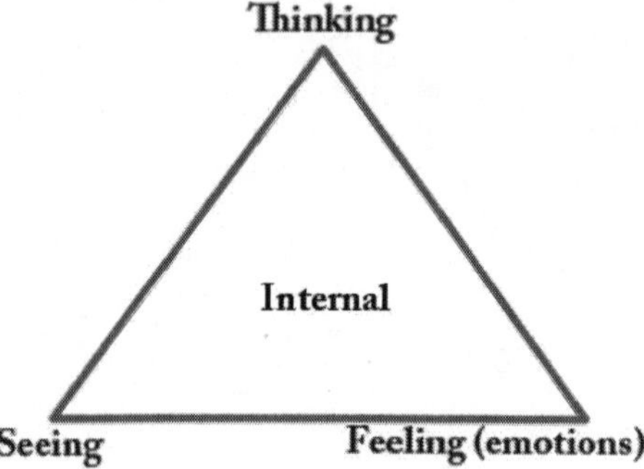

Fig. 16 Transient Self I

4. Choose a place that is clean and free from disturbance (people, telephones, noisy traffic etc.)

5. Sit in a firm but comfortable chair, ensuring that your spine is straight and that your head is balanced comfortably, without leaning too far forward or too far back.

6. Alternatively, lie down on the floor.

7. Relax, as described in Module 2

8. Focus on the following, ask yourself, 'What am I currently hearing, smelling, touching?'

9. Note what is taking place and its effect upon you. To what degree is this influence external or internal?

10. When it feels right, focus on what you are seeing (internally), feeling (emotionally) and thinking about. Explore the connections between sensory input and internal experience.

11. Consider the above in different time frames, for example, the previous hour, the previous 3 hours, or the whole day since waking.

Use your notebook to record the results and impression of this exercise.

Exercise 6 – Transient Self II

This exercise is similar to the previous exercise, but instead of considering the sensory and environmental impact upon what your thinking and how you are feeling, you are directed to observe and meditate upon the nature of experience in three modes (see Fig. 17).

The lowest triad illustrates the biological nature of experience via the senses, the second triad denotes the psychological dimension of experience via the chemistry of consciousness in our thoughts, imagination and feelings. The third alludes to the more permanent aspect of Self, in the application of the Will, the nature of memory and recall, and in the nature and function of intellect.

Three areas of interest arise in this exercise. The first is a growing awareness of these areas of activity and the second is the transient nature of that activity. Thirdly, there is a sense of an 'other' permanent sense of Self implicit in this field of experience, and it is the distillation of the permanent Self that is the main objective of this, and indeed, all of these exercises.

Use your notebook to record the results and impression of this exercise.

Module 4 – Controlled Imagining

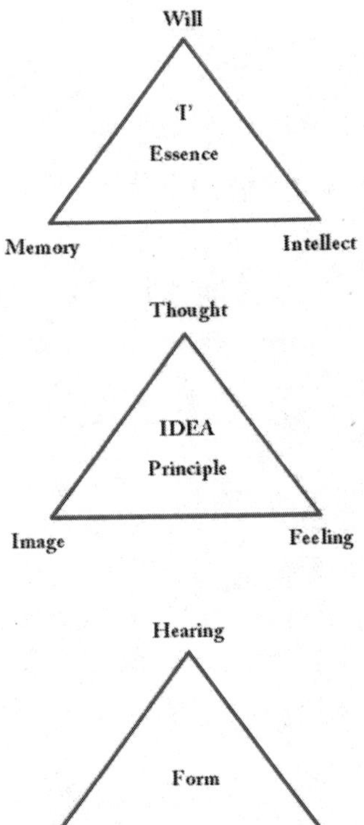

Fig. 17 Transient Self II

Module 5 – The Art of Meditation

Exercise 7 – Developing a concept of God

In the precincts of the sanctuary the main applicaion of meditation is in the labour of self-knowledge. In the development of this process the student will inevitably be confronted by the spiritual dimension of existence with a vast range possibilities.

At heart of the notion of spirituality rests the proposition of the existence of a God. A divine, absolute, sentient, omniscient being who created and continues to sustain the multi-dimensional universe we live in. It is probably true to say that more has been written about God than about any other subject.

Yet, for many of us the concept of God, assuming we have one, would have been formed in childhood, possibly through family and friends but more likely at school in cultural and religious lessons and in discussions with classmates and, arguably, it is a conception that has barely changed or developed since. Such a concept of God will often be anthropomorphic and quite naïve, a model in which God is created in Man's image. This model frequently generates challenging questions such as, 'Why suffering' or 'Why injustice'? Questions such as these are naturally paradoxical and consequently drive many to reject the spiritual basis of life altogether. Indeed, for many, the perceived reward and punishment model of the postmortem condition is completely abhorent, although for some it is reassuring.

Whether it be for the purpose of acceptance or rejection the student will at some point in their development need to evolve their own concept of God, of divinity, of the divine nature and of the relationship the human soul has with God.

Step 1 – The Concept of God

Define what you know about God, separating fact from fiction, what is actually taught as opposed to what you actually think.

Using the force-field analysis (see Fig. 8, p. 64), list what you know and what you don't know. Take your time, this is a slow process of distillation in which you may repeat the cycle of self-enquiry and reflection many times.

Step 2 – The Nature of God

This is best undertaken as a shared or group exericise. It is a complex exercise involving several stages of activity.

Stage I – Brainstorming (this can be undertaken individually or as a group exercise – see p. 65)

Stage II – Mind mapping (again, this may be an individual or group exercise – see pp. 66 – 67)

Stage III - Meditate on the findings of Stages I & II and record results in notebook (best undertaken as an individual exercise)

Step 3 – The Soul's Relationship with God

Stage I – (Individually) define what you believe your relationship with and to God actually is (record impressions in notebook)

Stage II – (Group session) discuss and compare with others (use a flip chart and the priority management matrix to record and apportion the different factors that arise)

Stage III – (Individually) meditate upon what emerged in previous stages and then record impressions and conclusions in notebook

Step 4 – Engaging with God

Stage I – (Group session) discuss and compare what you think the appropriate methods might be (use the flip chart to record conclusions)

Stage II - (Individually) Meditate upon what emerged in previous stages and then record impressions and conclusions in notebook.

Conclusion

(Individually) Gather together the results of Steps 1 – 4 and arange into an orderly form. Meditate upon the nature and results of your enquiry.

(Group Session) Discuss and compare with others. (use a flipchart and any other tool to arrange the thoughts and conclusions you have reached.

Note

In the language of spiritual alchemy, which is a language rooted in symbolism, this work (Steps 1 – 4) is a preparatory work that begins a process of 'separating' the truth from fiction, and then, 'extracting' the essential wisdom from the accumulated facts. It is a labour that requires patience and a willingness to sift and reflect upon the work at hand.

In this way a student acquires the 'insight' referred to on page 70 – a term that describes the ability to acquire a profound understanding of an object through the sustained concentration of the attention upon it. That concentration of the attention is likened to the controlled and sustained application of heat alluded to in many alchemical manuscripts.

Lectio Divina

The 'Way' or the 'Ladder'

A simple yet effective method that has been universally employed since ancient times is a method known simply as 'The way' or 'The ladder'. In more recent times, by which I mean from the sixth century onwards, it came to be known as *Lectio Divina* or 'divine reading', and as such was used specifically for the study of the Scriptures, but was also used as a basis for a graduated system of prayer. This method is an ancient spiritual discipline that was well known in the classical world. It consists of the slow repetitive reading of a passage of Scripture until it is known by heart, followed by meditating on its significance. Traditionally, the reading, or *lectio*, is read aloud with the emphasis upon the act of listening, and repeated time after time until the passage is known 'off by heart'. If the sacred text is to be read by another person it is important for those listening to repeat the words with their lips, under their breath as it were. This listening is no mere act of hearing; rather it is an act of attending with the whole of one's mind, engaging as much of one's being in the reading as possible, thereby cultivating the ability to perceive something of the soul of the text. This attending or listening extends into the act of thinking about the subject matter of the reading and as such is called *meditatio* or meditation.

The response to the *meditatio* was varied, but often took the form of spontaneous extemporary prayer, of communing with God or engaging in worship, singing hymns etc. This was known as *oratio*. At other times *Oratio* took the form of inspired writings that in some way related to the Lectio and *Meditatio*. Those who persevered with this discipline found that the *Oratio* subsided into a quiet state of rest in what has been described as the 'Presence' of God and was traditionally called *contemplatio* or contemplation. *Lectio Divina* is one of the oldest methods of prayer known to humanity. It is embodied in the works of Philo of Alexandria and is clearly expressed in the work of the Pseudo-Dionysius particularly in his book *On the Divine Names*. It was used extensively by the early Church, but was enshrined in the Rule of St. Benedict in the sixth century and became one of the distinctive features of monastic life.

The Four Stages of 'The Way'

Preparation:

Allow yourself sufficient time free from commitments to engage in this work without haste; an hour will do. Wear loose comfortable clothing. This should be done in a place set aside, ideally it should be done in a consecrated or sacred space, however, it may also be done in a domestic environment, but do choose a place that is clean and free from disturbance i.e. people, telephones, noisy traffic etc. Sit in a firm but comfortable chair, ensuring that the spine is straight and that the head is balanced comfortably, without leaning too far forward or backward.

Notes on Meditation

Stage 1

Having selected a short passage of text from the Scriptures, read it slowly over and over again (aloud if possible). Attend the mind to every word as it is read. Let your reading be slow and graceful, synchronizing your speech with your breathing, which should be gentle and easy. Continue in this manner for 10 – 15 minutes or until you know it 'off-by-heart'.

Stage 2

If you have been able to memorise the text then repeat it internally and silently, reflecting on its significance. Alternatively, a word or phrase may have attracted your attention, then reflect on the significance of that word or phrase in the context of the reading. Continue in this manner for as long as you are moved (e.g. for 10 – 30 minutes).

Stage 3

At some point in your reflections you may be inspired to write down or record your thoughts and impressions about the theme of your meditation. Alternatively, you may choose to express your experience in prayer, in song or perhaps in paint: some of the world's greatest spiritual prose was inspired in this exalted state.

Stage 4

There comes a time when the most natural thing to do is to be absolutely still, to allow the mind to fall silent. The experience may last only for a short moment or it may last much longer. Regardless of the time involved allow yourself the time to dwell without haste or anticipation in the sublime nature of the experience.

Note

Within the depths of that silence you may become aware of a profound sense of peace, a peace that slowly but surely embraces and permeates your soul as you rest therein. It is a 'peace that surpasseth all understanding'[1] and constitutes the first tangible experience of the Presence of the Divine. Abiding in that 'Presence' is the basis of true contemplation and the experience of it is the bedrock of unshakeable faith. It is with good reason considered in some schools to be the main objective of meditation.

Many have written concerning this state, and most concur in affirming that it is a state of being that emerges, as it were, as a gift from God by which the soul is enabled to mature and evolve in the spiritual life, and as such is beyond the manipulation of the discursive mind, whose only recourse is to be silent. The Pseudo-Dionysius, writing in the late fifth century, spoke of it in his book, *The Divine Names*, thus:

> Just as the senses can neither grasp nor perceive the things of the mind, just as representation and shape cannot take in the simple and the shapeless, just as corporal form cannot lay hold of the intangible and incorporeal, by the same standard of truth beings are surpassed by the infinity beyond being, intelligibles by that oneness which is beyond intelligence".[2]

---

1 Philippians 4: 7
2 *Divine Names* 588b

Notes on Meditation

Summary

The virtue of *Lectio Divina* is that as a method it is simple, safe and very adaptable, but do not be misled by its simplicity. *Lectio Divina* has been a central feature of the monastic approach to spiritual development from the earliest days of the Desert Communites of the Levant to the present time. There are many levels of understanding embedded within its simple formula that will emerge with the experience of using it over time.

For example, the practice of *Lectio Divina* is based upon listening to the words of Scripture, reflecting (meditating) upon what is heard, and responding to what what is derived from those reflections. Alternatively, it is possible to use an image or a diagram (such as a mandala or perhaps a stained glass window), in which case Stage 1 would require the student to focus upon the literal significance of the image or diagram. Stage 2 would require the student to consider the symbolism of the image or diagram, and to meditate upon the implications of that symbolism. Stage 3 would expect the student to articulate a response, either in writing or in some other form such as song or dance. Stage 4 would result in silence or contemplation in much the same way as *Lectio Divina.*

There follows a selection of readings from *The Dialogues of Plato*, the *Bhagavad Gita* and the *I Ching* that may be used as subjects for meditation in general. Some are from the *New Testament* and are suitable for *Lectio Divina*. They are offered merely as samples to serve as guides only. Students generally tend to follow a course best suited to their own taste.

Themes for Meditation

On Creation [from Plato's *Timaeus*[1]]

Let me tell you why the creator made this world of generation. He was good, and the good can never have any jealousy of anything. And being free from jealousy, he desired that all things should be as like himself as they could be. This is in the truest sense the origin of creation and of the world, as we shall do well in believing on the testimony of wise men: [30a]

...the creator, reflecting on the things which are by nature visible, found that no unintelligent creature taken as a whole could be fairer than the intelligent taken as a whole; and again that intelligence could not be present in anything which was devoid of soul. For which reason, when he was framing the universe, he put intelligence in soul, and soul in body, that he might be the creator of a work which was by nature fairest and best. On this wise, using the language of probability, we may say that the world came into being – a living creature truly endowed with soul and intelligence by the providence of God. [30b]

This being supposed, let us proceed to the next stage: In the likeness of what animal did the creator make the world? It would be an unworthy thing to liken it to any nature which exists As a part only; for nothing can be beautiful which is like any imperfect thing; but let us suppose the world to be the very image of that whole of which all other animals both individually and in their tribes are portions. For the original of the universe contains in itself all intelligible beings. For

1 *The Dialogues of Plato*, B. Jowett (Vol. 3) Clarendon Press, Oxford, 1953.

the Deity, intending to make this world like the fairest and most perfect of all intelligible beings, framed one visible animal comprehending within itself all other animals of a kindred spirit. [30c]

Now that which is created is of necessity corporeal, and also visible and tangible. [31b]

Now the creation took up the whole of each of the four elements; for the Creator compounded the world out of all the fire and all the water and all the air and all the earth, leaving no part of any of them nor any power of them outside. His intention was, in the first place, that the animal should be as far as possible a perfect whole and of perfect parts: secondly, that it should be one, leaving no remnants out of which another such world might be created. [32c]

He made the world one whole, having every part entire, and being therefore perfect and not liable to old age and disease. And he gave to the world the figure which was suitable and also natural. Now to the animal which was to comprehend all animals, the figure would be suitable which comprehends within itself all other figures. Wherefore he made the world in the form of a globe, round as from a lather, having the extremes in every direction equidistant from the centre, the most perfect and the most like itself of all figures. [33b]

But the movement suited to his spherical form was assigned to him, being of all the seven that which is most appropriate to mind and intelligence; and he was made to move in the same manner and on the same spot, within his own limits revolving in a circle. All the other six motions were taken away from him. [34a]

Such was the whole plan of the eternal God about the god who was to be; he made it smooth and even, having the surface in every direction equidistant from the centre, an body entire and perfect, and formed out of perfect bodies. And in the centre he put the soul, which he diffused throughout the body, making it also to be the exterior environment of it; and he made the universe a circle moving in a circle, one and solitary, yet by reason of its excellence able to converse with itself, and needing no other friendship or acquaintance. Having these purposes in view he created the world a blessed god. [34b]

...He made the soul in origin and excellence prior to and older that the body, to be the ruler and mistress, of whom the body was to be the subject. And he made her out of the following elements and on this wise:

From the being which is indivisible and unchangeable, and from that kind of being which is distributed among bodies, he compounded a third and intermediate kind of being

He did likewise with the Same and the Different, blending together the indivisible kind of each with that which is portioned out in bodies.

Then, taking the three new elements, he mingled them all into one form, compressing by force the reluctant and unsociable nature of the different into the same. When he had mingled them with [the intermediate kind of] being and out of the tree made one, he again divided this whole into as many portions as was fitting, each portion being a compound of the Same, the Different, and Being. [35a-b]

And he proceeded to divide after the following manner: [see 35 & 36] The series 1,2,3,4,9,8,27, can be arranged (As ancient commentators have pointed out) in the following diagram:

This entire compound (of the soul) he divided lengthways into two parts, which he joined to one another at the centre like the letter X, and bent them into a circular form, connecting them with themselves and each other at the point opposite to their original meeting point; and comprehending them in a uniform revolution upon the same axis, he made one the outer and the other the inner circle. Now the motion of the outer circle he called the motion of the Same, and the motion of the Other or diverse.

On the Kingdom of Heaven [from the *New Testament*[2]]

Seek first the kingdom of God. [Matt. 6 : 33]

And do not seek what you should eat or what you should drink, nor have an anxious mind. 'For all these things the nations of the world seek after, and your Father knows that you need these things.' But seek the kingdom of God and all these things shall be added to you.' [Luke 12 : 29 – 31]

The kingdom of God does not come with observation; nor will they say, 'see here!' or 'See there!' For indeed, the kingdom of God is within you. [Luke 17 : 20 – 21]

2 *Holy Bible,* New King James Version, Thomas Nelson, Nashville 1980

Turn within

But you, when you pray, go into your room, and when you have shut your door, pray to your Father who is in the secret place; and your Father who sees in secret will reward you openly. [Matthew 6 : 6]

Commune with God

Our Father in heaven,
Hallowed be Thy name.
Thy Kingdom come,
Thy will be done
On earth as it is in heaven.
Give us this day our daily bread,
And forgive us our debts,
As we forgive our debtors.
And lead us not into temptation,
But deliver us from evil.
For Thine is the kingdom and the power and the glory
Forever and ever Amen. [Matthew 6 : 9 – 13]

On the Interior Work [From the *Bhagavad Gita*[3]]

There was never a time when I did not exist, nor you, nor any of these kings. Nor is there any future in which we shall cease to be. Just as the dweller in this body passes through childhood, youth and old age, so at death he merely passes into another kind of body. [Yoga of Knowledge]

Bodies are said to die, but That which possesses the body is eternal. It cannot be limited, or destroyed. [Yoga of Knowledge]

---

3 *The Bhagavad Gita*, trans. Swami Prabhavananda & Christopher Isherwood, Phoenix House, London, 1947.

Worn out garments are shed by the body: worn out bodies are shed by the dweller within the body. New bodies are donned by the dweller, like garments. [Yoga of Knowledge]

This Atman cannot be manifested to the senses, or thought about by the mind. It is not subject to modification. [Yoga of Knowledge]

He who dwells within all living bodies remains forever indestructible. Therefore, you should never mourn for any one. [Yoga of Knowledge]

In this Yoga, the will is directed singly toward one ideal. When a man lacks this discrimination, his will wanders in all directions, after innumerable aims. [Yoga of Knowledge]

You Arjuna must overcome the three gunas. You must be free from the pairs of opposites. [Yoga of Knowledge]

You have the right to work, but for the work's sake only. You have no right to the fruits of the work. [Yoga of Knowledge]

Perform every action with your heart fixed on the Supreme Lord. Renounce attachment to the fruits. [Yoga of Knowledge]

In the calm of self-surrender you can free yourself from the bondage of virtue and vice during this very life. [Yoga of Knowledge]

When your intellect has cleared itself of its delusions, you will become indifferent to the results of all action, present or future. At present your intellect is bewildered by conflicting interpretations of the scriptures. When it can rest, steady and undistracted, in contemplation of the Atman, then you will reach union with the Atman. [Yoga of Knowledge]

Thinking about sense-objects will attach you to sense-objects. [Yoga of Knowledge]

When he has no lust, no hatred, a man walks safely among the things of lust and hatred. [Yoga of Knowledge]

On the Interior Work [*From the I Ching*]

As the gentle wind shapes the clouds, so the wise man refines his bearing. [Hex. 9]

As the sun sheds light on good and evil, so the wise man curbs evil and furthers good. He thereby fulfils the will of heaven. [Hex. 14]

Clarity within and quiet without: the wise man has time for meditation. [Hex. 22]

Within the mountain: heaven, Hidden riches. So the wise man studies the sayings of old and the deeds of the past to enrich himself. [Hex. 26]

As a lake rises above the treetops in extraordinary times of flood: so the wise man in extraordinary times, is unconcerned if he stands alone. Even if he has to renounce the world, he is as undaunted as joyousness. [Hex. 28]

As water flows on, on, on to reach its goal, so the wise man walks in lasting virtue. [Hex. 29]

The great man perpetuates his brightness and illuminates all quarters of the world. [Hex. 30]

As the sun rises over the earth, thus does the wise man brighten his virtue. In 'Devotion to Great Clarity' is a path. [Hex. 35]

As the light sinks into the earth, so does the wise man live with the world: he veils his light, yet still he shines. [Hex. 36]

As a lake below enriches a mountain above; as decrease below gives increase above; thus does the wise man curb his passions. [Hex. 41]

The lake is dried up, exhausted. When adverse fate befalls him, the wise man stakes his life on following his will. [Hex. 47]

As a mountain keeps still within itself, thus a wise man does not permit his will to stray beyond his situation. [Hex. 52]

As thunder stirs the surface of a lake, so a wise man sees transitory movement in the light of the eternity of the end. [Hex. 54]

As two lakes join to replenish each other, so the wise man joins with his friends to discuss and practise the truths of life. [Hex. 58]

Fire and water are opposites by nature, so a wise man differentiates with care. He separates things in order to unite them, that each should find its proper place. [Hex. 64]

On the Interior Work [from the *New Testament*]

God is a Spirit: and they that worship Him must worship Him in Spirit and in Truth. [John 4: 24,]

Verily, verily, I say unto thee, except a man be born of water and of the Spirit, he cannot enter into the kingdom of God. That which is born of the flesh is flesh; and that which is born of the Spirit is spirit. Marvel not that I said unto thee, ye must be born again. The wind bloweth where it listeth, and thou hearest the sound thereof, but canst not tell whence it cometh, and whither it goeth: so is every one that is born of the Spirit. [John 3: 5 – 8]

It is the Spirit that quickeneth; the flesh profiteth nothing: the words that I speak unto you, they are spirit, and they are life. [John 6: 63]

Behold, the kingdom of God is within you. [Luke 17: 21]

Know ye not that ye are the temple of God, and that the Spirit of God dwelleth in you? [1 Cor. 3: 16]

I and my Father are one. [John 10: 30]

I am the way, the truth, and the life: no man cometh unto the Father, but by me. [John 14: 6]

I am the door: by me if any man enter in, he shall be saved, and shall go in and out, and find pasture. [John 10: 9]

My kingdom is not of this world. [John 18: 36]

Believe me that I am in the Father, and the Father in me: or else believe me for the very works' sake. [John 14: 11)]

On Faith

And Jesus rebuked the demon, and it came out of him; and the child was cured from that very hour. Then the disciples came to Jesus privately and said, 'Why could we not cast it out?' So Jesus said to them, 'Because of your unbelief; for assuredly, I say to you, if you have faith as a mustard seed, you will say to this mountain, 'Move from here to there,' and it will move; and nothing will be impossible for you. However, this kind does not go out except be prayer and fasting.' [Matt. 17: 18 – 21]

When Jesus departed from there, two blind men followed Him, crying out and saying, 'Son of David have mercy on us!' And when He had come into the house, the blind men came to Him. And Jesus said to them, 'Do you believe that I am able to do this?' They said to Him, 'Yes, Lord.' Then He touched their eyes, saying, 'According to your faith let it be to you.' And their eyes were opened. [Matt. 9: 27 – 30]

He said to them, 'Let us cross to the other side.' Now when they had left the multitude, they took Him along in the boat as He was. And other little boats were also with Him. And a great windstorm arose, and the waves beat into the boat, so that it was already filling. But He was in the stern, asleep on a pillow. And they awoke Him and said to Him, 'Teacher, do You not care that we are perishing?' Then He arose and rebuked the wind, and said to the sea, 'Peace, be still.' And the wind ceased and there was a great calm. But He said to them, 'Why are you so fearful? How is it that you have no faith?'[Mark 4: 35 – 40]

So Jesus answered and said to them, 'Have faith in God. For assuredly, I say to you, whoever says to this mountain, "Be removed and be cast into the sea," and does not doubt in his heart, but believes that those things he says will be done, he will have whatever he says. Therefore I say to you whatever things you ask when you pray, believe that you receive them, and you will have them.' [Mark 11: 22 – 24]

He who is faithful in what is least is faithful also in much; and he who is unjust in what is least is unjust also in much. Therefore if you have not been faithful in the unrighteous mammon, who will commit to your trust the true riches? And if you have not been faithful in what is another man's, who will give you what is your own? [Luke 16: 10 – 12]

On Love

You have heard that it was said, 'You shall love your neighbour and hate your enemy.' But I say to you, love your enemies, bless those who curse you, do good to those who hate you, and pray for those who spitefully use you and persecute you, that you may be sons of your Father in heaven; for He makes His sun rise on the evil and on the good, and sends rain on the just and on the unjust. [Matt. 5: 43 – 45]

Then one of the scribes came, and having heard them reasoning together, perceiving that He had answered them well, asked Him, 'Which is the first commandment of all?' Jesus answered him, 'The first of all the commandments is: "Hear O Israel, the Lord our God, the Lord is One. And you shall love the Lord your God with all your heart, with all your soul, with all your minds, and with all your strength. This is the first commandment. And the second, like it, is this: 'You shall love your neighbour as yourself. There is no other commandment greater than these.' [Mark 12: 28 – 31]

No servant can serve two masters; for either he will hate the one and love the other, or else he will be loyal to the one and despise the other. You cannot serve God and mammon. [Luke 16: 13]

As the Father loved Me, I also have loved you; abide in My love. If you keep My commandments, you will abide in My love, just as I have kept My Father's commandments and abide in His love. These things I have spoke to you, that My joy may remain in you, and that your joy may be full. This is My commandment, that you love one another as I have loved you. [John 15: 9 – 12]

O righteous Father! The world has not known You, but I have known You; and these have known that You sent Me. And I have declared to them Your name, and will declare it, that the love with which You loved Me may be in them, and I in them. [John. 17: 25-26]

Module 6 – Therapeutic Meditation

Therapeutic meditation is not meditation in the traditional sense of being a discipline of mind control. It is a method of establishing health affirming thought-patterns and ideas and of generating endorphins (see p. 18). As such it is a powerful tool that may be used in the process of restoring good health in body, mind and soul.

Environment

A central feature of this method is the preparation of the environment so that it is conducive towards a peaceful atmosphere and capable of generating a positive and restful sensory experience. With this in mind the environment, (indoors or out) should be made comfortably warm, quiet and peaceful. It should also be free of clutter and have a focal point that is beautiful and calming to look at. It goes without saying that 'beauty is in the eye of the beholder', therefore any focal point for group activity requires some consideration of the sensitivities of the people involved.

The use of gentle music, soft lighting (candles, for example), essential oils, perfume or incense to introduce an additional sense of harmony may be appropriate. (A water feature or gently sounding wind chimes may also be advantageous.)

Notes on Meditation

Posture

Sitting upright is not essential (as in a traditional method such as *Lectio Divina*). A more appropriate posture might be achieved by reclining in an easy chair or on a sun lounger, or even upon a bed. Wear comfortable clothing

A favourite calming drink (e.g. camomile tea) should be available if necessary.

The intention of the exercise

This exercise is designed to be a co-ordinated/led meditation. The co-ordinator or leader should make suitable preparations, including the creation of a script to guide the meditation. (see notes) It may be the case that spiritual healing (laying on of hands) is to be a feature of the exercise. If that is so then the consensus of those involved must be acquired before beginning, and the appropriate resources made ready.

Duration

The duration of the meditation will be determined by several factors. The first will be the purpose itself, the second may be the health of any participant who might be recuperating from illness or surgery. Another factor could be the personal disposition of the participant, or simply the time available. Whatever the case may be, the duration of the exercise should be no less than 15 and no more than 60 minutes. This exercise may be repeated if necessary several times during the course of the day (e.g. morning, noon and evening).

Module 6 –Therapeutic Meditation

Method

Step 1
Play gentle music in the background and if appropriate introduce a pleasant smell (perfume or incense) to the environment.

Step 2
Reclining in an easy chair or sun lounger and engage in Relaxation Method 2 (Module 2). If approriate, play the pre-recorded script designed to assist the meditation, otherwise read slowly, pacing the flow of words and tone of voice to suit the text and those partaking. (this may be discussed prior to the meditation)

Step 3
Use the imagination to recall or to create a beautiful, calm, environment such as a beach or woodland glade, or perhaps a garden or favourite room. Imagine that you are in that environment, lying on the warm sand of the beach, or on the warm grass of a woodland glade, or reclining on a sun-lounger in your garden or favourite room, without any sense of time or need to be anywhere else.

Step 4
Allow yourself the freedom to enjoy the environment in which you find yourself, allowing the music and perfume or incense to fill you with good feelings.

Step 5
Following the controlled imagination exercise in Module 4, imagine your breath as sunlight flowing into the centre of your being and flowing out from that centre as waves of life-giving light flooding into every cell and fibre of your body.

Imagine that light flowing from your centre along your arms and legs and up through your torso into and through your head, entering every cell of every finger, every toe and into every hair follicle. Imagine that light flooding your entire body with warmth, with well-being and with health and vitality.

Step 6
Allow the experience of well-being to sink deep into you, embrace it and allow it to embrace you, to wash away tiredness, discomfort, negative emotions, pain and disease just as wax melts before the flame, or the early morning mist dispersing before the rising sun.

Step 7
If appropriate, a short reading may be introduced here to assist the meditation. Alternatively, this may be an ideal moment for the 'laying on of hands' or some other healing method.

Step 8
When the reading or 'laying on of hands' is finished allow time for reflection about the subject matter involved (10 – 30 minutes).

Step 9

Articulate (reading or singing), or play the predetermined affirmations that are conducive to the theme of the meditation.

Step 10

As in Step 5, imagine your breath as sunlight flowing into the centre of your being and flowing out from that centre as waves of life-giving light flooding into every cell and fibre of your body, establishing peace, health and vitality.

Finally, stand and finish with engaging in some gentle stretching exercises.

Notes

Therapeutic meditation is not designed to be a religious or spiritual process, although it may function as a platform or vehicle for spiritual healing. The key to this method is in the title, 'therapeutic', which indicates that the underlying purpose is the healing of those participating. The strenuous demands on the body and mind make *Lectio Divina* generally unsuitable for this kind of therapy, which may involve people who are very ill or recovering from a serious illness. Therapeutic meditation rests upon establishing a peaceful state of mind in participants so that a more effective healing may take place. It is a method designed to generate Endorphins and to develop and establish health affirming thought-patterns and ideas.

Notes on Meditation

Step 1

Music The choice of music is important; therefore it is worthwhile securing agreement about the music used or not used.

Candles Some people dislike candles, scented or not, and it is important to reach an agreement about their use.

Incense Some people react badly to smoke, or anything that suggests church incense. An oil burner, the kind where the essential oil floats on water heated by a tea-light, is generally less likely to evoke a negative response.

Step 2

Easy chairs – are generally more readily available but use a sun lounger if possible as they are more comfortable. In either case provide small covers for participants' convenience.

Relaxation method – This should be scripted and read by the co-ordinator. It is important that this stage should not be hurried.

Step 3 – 6

Script – Steps 3 – 6 should also be read from a script in a gentle and unhurried manner.

Step 7

This is an opportunity to insert a short meaningful reading that has a bearing on the purpose of the meditation. It should be read by a person other than the co-ordinator. Alternatively, this may be the ideal moment for the 'laying on of hands' or some other healing method.

Step 8

Some people are unaccustomed to extended periods of silence. For such people prolonged silence may induce a state of anxiety rather than peace; therefore, the co-ordinator should be mindful of each participant, bearing in mind that a short period of quality reflection is preferred above a longer period of anxious reflection.

Step 9

Affirmations An affirmation is an assertion. Some affirmations are conscious assertions such as 'I like tea!' However many affirmations are deeply embedded within the mind and to all intents and purposes we are unconscious of their role in our lives.

All affirmations influence our thinking and clearly many of our thoughts are negative. Unfortunately, every negative thought or word constitutes a negative affirmation, and because we are frequently emotionally attached to them we find them easier to live with. They influence the way we think and feel about things, therefore, replacing them with more constructive beliefs and ideas through the use of positive affirmations will effect positive change in our everyday life.

Positive affirmations are typically short positive statements used to replace negative beliefs and attitudes and the more determined the individual is to make changes and let go of negative thoughts and attitudes the more effective the affirmation will be. Designing and using an affirmation is more than constructing a sentence and repeating it. It is a process that begins with developing an awareness of our thinking and the attitudes that condition our everyday life.

Start by giving some time to thinking about the changes you want to make in your life. Use the exercises in Module 3 to prioritise the areas of your life you would like to improve. Construct a selection of positive statements for each. They should be positive and in the present tense; therefore focus on what you actually want to achieve rather than on what you do not want.

An effective way of using an affirmation is to utter it out loud (privately of course) or sing it. A general affirmation used as a musical round within a group of participants is a very powerful tool. Another effective way of keeping an affirmation at the forefront of the mind is to write it down; leave a note in a conspicuous place where you will notice it throughout the day.

Examples of Affirmations

- I rejoice in the light of the morning, in the warmth of the noonday sun; I rejoice in the fall of evening and in the deeps of the peaceful night.

- My body heals quickly and easily
  My mind heals quickly and easily
  My soul heals quickly and easily.

- I am at peace with myself and the world.

- I trust in life, in the light and in the power of love.

Conclusion

Having come thus far it is now time to rest the pen. It is tempting to continue writing, but to do so would be an extravagance as we have introduced more than enough material necessary for effective meditation, and sufficient information to engage the most enquiring of minds. Indeed, by engaging with these modules students will have begun a journey of self-knowledge that will take them far beyond the life of the senses experienced in this mortal frame, and they may be justifiably pleased to have done so. Concerning which, on a personal note, when I joined the Order of Dionysis and Paul I was in due course introduced to the discipline of meditation. After some years had passed I began to understand that meditation is far more than a method or technique. I recognised that the term 'meditation' was really more of a sign, hung upon a door as it were, a door giving entrance to the whole spectrum of the spiritual life. I then realised that meditation never was the objective but the means by which the soul may enter into an interior spiritual kingdom. Granted, it is a little difficult at first, even frustrating at times; but, like riding a bike, it soon becomes second nature.

The work set out in this book is provided to assist the student in to enter that kingdom, and it is hoped by now that it is quite clear to the reader that without learning something about one's own biology, and developing the means to either control or transcend its influence, effective meditation and gaining entrance to the inner kingdom of the soul will always be beyond one's reach. It is with this in mind that the preliminary work set out in the first four modules was designed. Those who persevere with the tried and tested exercises provided in these modules will inevitably make progress in effective meditation.

However, there is one other factor that does need to be taken into consideration, and that is motivation. What is it that motivates a person to engage in the discipline of meditation? For some it simply may be the need to achieve a degree of mental control, which is in itself a worthy motive. However, for others it may be a response to an inner calling, a spiritual urge that cannot be ignored, an irrepressible impulse to discover the meaning of existence and the source of one's being. This need 'to know' the purpose and meaning of life beyond the secular views of society and the exponents of the sciences is compelling, and those who are compelled by it are driven to follow what appears to others as a spiritual way of life.

This compulsion is something that all of humanity share in common, although many if not most of us channel it into exploring the material world of the senses – which is no bad thing. Nevertheless, there are still significant numbers of people who commit themselves to the challenging work of self-knowledge, because discovering answers to the meaning of existence, including questions such as, Who am I? What am I? Why am I here? Where am I going? Why suffering? Is there a God? What is God? is important to them. And these are only a few of the more obvious questions that have been asked by every generation, including our own, and will probably continue to be asked by the generations yet to come as the answers provided by the secular world are for various reasons insufficient, or perhaps it is simply because 'knowing' is not the same as rationally comprehending a fact.

For the members of the Order of Dionysis and Paul the spiritual life is imperative; consequently, meditation is an important part of Order life, providing, as it does, both a platform for making sense of the secular world and a stepping stone into the interior domain of the soul. In this interior world, meditation, particularly as described in these notes on meditation, provides the means of harnessing the faculties of both body and soul and using them in the work of the spiritual life. This forms in its own time another platform or stepping stone that enables the soul to enter into the deep stillness of contemplation.

There are countless methods and techniques of meditation available in the world today. I have provided one from the Rituale of the Order. As you have discovered it is called *Lectio Divina*. I could have provided others, but such an act would have been superfluous because *Lectio Divina* is a very adaptable platform that will comfortably accommodate many variations in technique and method, indeed, the therapeutic meditation method is simply a secular variation of *Lectio Divina*. Furthermore, unlike many other disciplines, to be skilled in the meditative arts does not require a wide knowledge of different methods and techniques of meditation; quite the opposite, as a matter of fact. One good method is sufficient.

On these terms within the Order of Dionysis and Paul it is a matter of principle that members become proficient with one discipline before considering engaging with another. This is because the degree of proficiency required, especially where meditation is concerned, may take many years of practice before there is sufficient maturity of understanding to move from one discipline to another. This may not be the case for every student, but it remains true that time and practice is important in any discipline, especially when engaging with the interior life of the soul.

As a novice I wanted to experience everything at once, so my teacher gave me a fable to consider regarding this very subject. It is as follows: a person walked across a meadow full of long grass. Upon looking back there was no visible sign of the crossing, but after walking back and forth a few times it was clear where this person had crossed. After many more crossings a trail had been clearly made through the meadow. So it is with meditation. After engaging in the same method for a considerable time the pathway into the soul is established and there is no real need to create another. Upon grasping that point I applied myself to the work set before me and continue still in developing my understanding of the interior life of the soul.

Thus ends a brief introduction to the meditational work of the Order of Dionysis and Paul. The study of this subject is not a short-term commitment but a life-time's work that unfolds according to the inspiration and guidance of the Holy Spirit.

Reccomended Reading

George Appleton, Edit., *The Oxford Book of Prayer*, Oxford University Press, 1985

Allan Armstrong ODP, *The Secret Garden of the Soul*, Imagier Publishing, Bristol 2008

Allan Armstrong ODP, *Aspects of the Spiritual Life*, Anyioch Papers, Bristol 2010

Ignatius Brianchaninov, , *On the Prayer of Jesus,* trans. Father Lazarus, Ibis Press, Maine, 2006

The Complete Book of Christian Prayer, the Continuum Publishing Company, New York, 1997

Stephen Covey, *Seven Habits of Highly Effective People*, Freepress, London, 1989

R.A. Gilbert, *The Elements of Mysticism,* Element Books, Shaftsbury, Dorset, 1991

Guigo II, *Ladder of Monks,* trans. Edmund Colledge OSA & James Walsh SJ, Cistercian Publications, Kalamazoo, 1979

A. Hamman, Edit. *Early Christian Prayers*, trans. Walter Mitchell, Longmans, Green, London 1961

Holy Bible, New King James Version

B. Jowett, *Dialogues of Plato*, Oxford University Press, 1953

Patrick O'Connor, Edit., *The Prayers of Man, from Primitive Peoples to Present Times*, Trans. Rex Benedict, William Heinemann, London, 1962

Rudolph Otto, *The Idea of the Holy*, trans. John W. Harvey, Oxford University Press, London, 1923

Pseudo-Dionysius, The Complete Works, trans. Colm Luibeid and Paul Rorem, SPCK, London 1987

Isherwood C. & Swami Prabhavananda, Trans. *The Bhagavad Gita*,

C. Isherwood & Swami Prabhavananda, trans. *Upanishads, Breath of the Eternal*

Richard Wilhelm, trans. *The I Ching*, Routledge & Kegan Paul London 1951

Frances A. Yates, *The Art of Memory*, Routledge & Kegan Paul, London, 1966

Arthur Edward Waite, *The Way of Divine Union*, William Rider & Son, London, 1915

INDEX

A

abdomen 47, 51
academic studies 78
acupuncture 19
adrenaline 31, 32, 34, 38
adrenals 31
affirmation 121, 122
air 75
Alexandria 22, 99
allegorical 22
Alpha wave 41
ambient music 9, 16
amino acids 32, 72
Anabaptist 11
analgesic 18, 35
analytical psychology 18
ancestor worship 17
ankles 46, 50, 51
antidepressants 35
antioxidant 35
anxiety 34, 37, 38, 39, 40, 42, 43, 121
apathy 34
archetypal 15, 16, 76
architecture 60
astral projection 16
attention 22, 23, 42, 43, 46, 47, 48, 49, 50, 51, 52, 53, 54, 69, 70, 88, 100
autan 81
autonomic nervous system 27

B

beach 59, 117
Beatles 9
behaviourism 18
Berger, Hans 41
Berlin Wall 60
Beta wave 41
Bible 21, 106, 127
biochemistry 23
biological vii, 20, 26, 75, 77, 78, 80, 92
biological imperatives 77
biological programming 77
biologist 72
blood pressure 28, 31, 32, 35, 80
bloodstream 31, 32, 35, 36
brain 18, 27, 31, 38, 41, 75, 80
brainstorming 63, 65, 95
brain waves 41
breathing 15, 31, 40, 41, 44, 46, 49, 50, 51, 52, 53, 70, 88, 100
Buddhist 15

C

calcium 31, 36
calories 36
calves 46, 51
candles 115, 120
Catholic 11
cell 28, 32, 36, 71, 72, 76, 118, 119
Celtic saints 10

chair 16, 45, 46, 90, 99, 116, 117
channelling 18
chemicals 30
chemistry of consciousness viii, 70, 77, 79, 89, 92
Christ 20
Christian 10, 11, 20, 128
cipher 22
circadian 31
clairvoyance 24
classical world 98
clenched fists 55
climate 80
communication 55
Compline 11, 12
concentrate 23, 54, 70, 88
concentration 23, 26, 34, 69, 70
concept 61, 95
contemplative vii
co-ordinator 116, 120, 121
cortisol 31, 32, 34
cube 57
curriculum 67
cycles 46, 51, 52, 53, 81
cytoplasm 72

D

depression 34
Desert Communites 102
Desert Fathers 10
design 62
Dharma 20
dhikr 9, 12
digestion 28
Divine Light 76
DNA 72

E

Earth 75, 76, 80, 81
Earth's core 76
ecological 9
economic 9
education 63, 78
electrical 41, 72
electric potential 72
electro-magnetic 76
emergency 43
endocrine glands 31
endorphins 18, 35, 115, 119
energy 30, 31, 32, 36, 50, 51, 52, 53, 55, 72, 73, 75, 76, 79, 80, 82
enzymes 72
epinephrine 32
esoteric 16, 22
euphoric 35
Europe 16, 17
existence 20, 21, 22, 24, 94, 124
eyes 15, 38, 48, 54, 55, 57, 58, 59, 112

F

face 48, 52
Far East 16
fear 34
feet 38, 46, 50, 51
festivals 9
fight/flight mechanism 27
fingers 48, 54
fire 75, 110
flip-chart 66
focusing 65

Index

folklore 81
force-field 64
forefinger 54
forest glade 59
foundation 69, 76
four elements 75, 104
France 11, 81
free association 65
frequencies 43
Freud 18
fulcrum 44
function 62

G

garden 22, 128
gaze 57
genes 72
geometry 57, 58, 59
glucagon 32, 34
glucose 31, 32, 34
God vii, 9, 10, 11, 12, 19, 94, 95, 96, 99, 101, 103, 105, 106, 107, 111, 113, 114, 125
Golden Dawn, 16
gonads 31
Greek islands 9
Guru Mahesh Yogi 9

H

head 48
healing 116, 118, 119, 120
heart disease 35
heart rate 28, 31
Hermetic 16, 17
hormones 28, 30, 31, 32, 34, 35,
hyperthyroidism 36
hypothalamus 27, 28, 30, 31, 80

I

I Ching 102, 109, 127
idea 23, 61, 65, 67
image-making 56, 57
imagination 15, 16, 18, 24, 25, 39, 40, 41, 65, 67, 82, 92
immune system 18, 31, 35
in-breath 50, 51, 52, 53
incense 9, 115, 117, 120
India 9
influx 76
insight 21, 24
insight 70
insomnia 34
inspiration 23, 58, 65
instinct 77
insulin 31, 32, 34
integrated systems 75
ions 72, 81

J

jaw 48, 52, 55
Jesus Prayer 12
Jung 18

K

kidneys 36
knees 47

L

ladder 98
Lakhosky, Georges 72

laying on of hands 116, 118, 120
leaf 57
Lectio Divina 98, 99, 102, 116, 119, 125
Levant 102
life-skills 54
liver 31, 38
lymph 75

M

magical 16, 25
magnetic field 76
manufactured object 58
materialism 18
matter 20, 23, 26, 39, 40, 63, 73, 74, 75, 98, 118, 126
meditation vii, 1, 9, 15, 24, 44, 79, 91, 94, 101, 103, 115, 119, 122, 125
melas 9
melatonin 31, 35
membrane 72
Mennonite 13
mental acuity 32
metabolism 30, 31, 32, 35, 36, 81
metaphorical 22, 77
microcosmic 75
micro-system 72
mind vii, 15, 16, 18, 20, 21, 22, 23, 24, 25, 26, 44, 56, 57, 59, 60, 65, 67, 70, 76, 77, 98, 100, 101, 104, 106, 108, 115, 119, 121, 122, 124
mind control 15, 20, 24, 25, 115
mind maps 62, 63, 68
mind's eye 56, 57, 59, 60, 77
mission vii
modelling 62
molecular 26
monastic 12, 99, 102
mood 31, 34, 60
Moon 81
moral values 9
morphine 35
mundane world 78
muraqaba 9
muscles 31, 32, 38, 46, 47, 48, 49, 51, 52, 53, 75
music 9, 16, 115, 117, 120
musical 58, 122
musical round 122

N

natural cycle 23
natural form 57, 58
natural world 23, 79, 80
neck 36, 48, 52, 54
negative anticipation 37
night prayer 11
Noradrenaline 32, 34
nostrils 45, 49, 50, 69
notion 61, 67, 94
nucleus 72
nutrients 28

O

object-focussed 54
objectives 62
ocean 76, 77, 80
ocean currents 80

Index

omniscient 94
opiates 35
Order of Dionysis and Paul vii, viii, 11, 123
organelles 72
organic molecules 72
organs 30, 31, 32, 38, 72, 75
oriental religions 15
Orthodox 11
oscillating circuit 72
out-breath 51, 52, 53
ovaries 31
oxygen 36, 38

P

pain regulators 35
pancreas 31
parathormone 36
parathyroid 31, 36
PARDeS 22
Philo Judaeus 22
philosophies 15
phosphate 31
phospholipids 72
photons 76
pineal 31, 34
pituitary 30, 32, 35
placenta 32
planning 62
poem 58
polypeptide 34
populist 10
positive ions 81
prayer vii, 12, 127, 128
precincts 20, 23, 79, 94
Presence of God vii
priorities 62
priority management matrix 64, 66
profound stillness 24
projection 16, 62
proposition 61
protein 18
Protestant 11
Prozac 35
Pseudo-Dionysius 99, 101, 127
psycho-dynamic vii
purpose 62

Q

Quaker 10

R

relationship skills 78
relaxation 15, 16, 19, 20, 26, 28, 40, 41, 43, 44, 49, 53, 54, 55, 69, 70, 88
reproduction 32, 35, 77
rhythm 49, 53
riding a bike 123
RNA 72
Rosicrucian 17
rumours 37

S

sacred texts 20, 21
sadhu 15
sanctuary 20, 23, 79
schools 16, 17, 23, 24, 25, 101
scientific 31
Scotland 9
script 116, 117, 120

Scripture 11, 98, 102
seasons 23, 80, 81
secular vii, 10, 19, 124, 125
self-enquiry 19, 95
self-esteem 34
self-knowledge viii, 15, 19, 21, 24, 25, 69, 79, 123, 124
sensations 69, 70
serotonin 31, 34
sexual development 31
shallow breathing 40
Shamanism 16, 17
shiatsu 19
Sirocco 81
skeleton 75
sleep/wake cycle 31
solar flares 81
solar plexus 47, 51, 52, 53
solar system 76
somatostatin 34
soul vii, viii, 78, 79, 95, 96, 98, 101, 103, 105, 106, 114, 123, 125
speech 55
sphere of sensation 75, 76
spherical 56
spiritual director vii
spiritual evolution 15
Spiritualism 16, 17
spiritual life 10, 79, 101, 123, 125
statue 60
stone 57, 125
stress 18, 26, 28, 37, 39, 43
Sufi 9, 12
sugar 31, 38
Sun 76, 80, 81
sunlight 80, 117, 119
sun lounger 116, 117, 120
sunspot 81
survival 28, 77
sympathetic nervous system 27, 28, 37, 40

T

T3 35
T4 35
Taizé 11
tea-light 120
tension 26, 37, 43, 50, 55
testes 31
tetrahedron 57
Theosophical Society 17
therapeutic 15, 19, 24, 25, 119
therapeutic meditation 115, 119, 125
thighs 47
thinking faculty 61
thoughts 63, 65, 66, 69, 77, 78, 88, 92, 97, 100, 121
thymus 31
thyroid 31, 35, 36
thyroxine 35
Tibetan Buddhists 9
Timaeus 103
tiny dot 56
tipis 9
tongue 49, 52, 55
traditional meditation 16, 19,

20, 22, 24, 25
triad 92
triiodthyronine 35
tryptophan 35

U

universe 94, 103, 105
Upanishads 20, 127

V

Vedanta 20
Vedas 20
village green 60
vision 31, 54, 55

W

Arthur Edward Waite 22, 128
Water 75
way, the 98
well-being 18, 19, 35, 81, 118
Western esotericism 16, 17
whiteboard 66
worry 37, 42, 53

Y

Yoga 16, 107, 108, 109
yurts 9